THE PENGUIN CLASSICS

FOUNDER EDITOR (1944–64): E. V. RIEU
Present Editors: Betty Radice and Robert Baldick

LAO TZU
TAO TE CHING

TRANSLATED
WITH AN
INTRODUCTION
BY

D. C. LAU

PENGUIN BOOKS

BALTIMORE · MARYLAND

INTRODUCTION

The *Lao tzu* has had an influence on Chinese thought through the ages out of all proportion to its length. It is often referred to as 'the book of five thousand characters', though, in fact, in most versions it is slightly longer than that. It is a short work even allowing for the fact that ancient Chinese was a very concise language and that the particular style in which it was written is more often than not succinct to the point of obscurity. If the *Lao tzu* is widely read in China as *the* classic in the thought of Taoism,* it is no less well known to the West through a long line of translators. In English alone there are well over thirty translations. The *Lao tzu* is, without a doubt, by far the most frequently translated work in Chinese, but unfortunately it cannot be said that it has been best served by its numerous translators, as the nature of the work attracted many whose enthusiasm for Eastern mysticism far outstripped their acquaintance with Chinese thought or even with the Chinese language.

The text of the *Lao tzu* is divided into two books. This was done probably simply to conform to the statement in the biography of Lao Tzu that he wrote a work *in two books* at the request of the Keeper of the Pass. At any rate, the division into two books goes at least as far back as the first century A.D. We have reason to believe that the present division into eighty-one chapters – thirty-seven in Book I and forty-four in Book II – also goes back to that time. By the end of the second century A.D., the work was also known by the alternative title of the *Tao te ching*. More specifically, Book I was known as the *Tao ching*, and Book II the *Te ching*. This practice seems to have

* For Chinese terms, proper names, and titles of books, see Glossary.

no more foundation than the mere fact that the first word in Book I is *tao* while in Book II the first word (discounting the adjective *shang* which has no special significance) is *te*.

The traditional view is that the *Lao tzu* was written by a man named Lao Tzu who was an older contemporary of Confucius (551–479 B.C.). The *locus classicus* of this tradition is the biography of Lao Tzu in the *Shih chi* (*Records of the Historian*), the earliest general history of China, written at the beginning of the first century B.C. by Ssu-ma Ch'ien:

Lao Tzu was a native of the Ch'ü Jen Hamlet in the Li Village of Hu Hsien in the State of Ch'u. His surname was Li, his personal name was Erh and he was styled Tan. He was the Historian in charge of the archives in Chou.

When Confucius went to Chou to ask to be instructed in the rites by him, Lao Tzu said, 'What you are talking about concerns merely the words left by people who have rotted along with their bones. Furthermore, when a gentleman is in sympathy with the times he goes out in a carriage, but drifts with the wind when the times are against him. I have heard it said that a good merchant hides his store in a safe place and appears to be devoid of possessions, while a gentleman, though endowed with great virtue, wears a foolish countenance. Rid yourself of your arrogance and your lustfulness, your ingratiating manners and your excessive ambition. These are all detrimental to your person. This is all I have to say to you.'

On leaving, Confucius told his disciples, 'I know a bird can fly, a fish can swim, and an animal can run. For that which runs a net can be made; for that which swims a line can be made; for that which flies a corded arrow can be made. But the dragon's ascent into heaven on the wind and the clouds is something which is beyond my knowledge. Today I have seen Lao Tzu who is perhaps like a dragon.'

Lao Tzu cultivated the way and virtue, and his teachings aimed at self-effacement. He lived in Chou for a long time, but seeing its decline he departed; when he reached the Pass, the Keeper there was pleased and said to him, 'As you are about to leave the world behind, could you write a book for my sake?' As a result, Lao Tzu wrote a work in two books, setting out the meaning of the way and virtue in some five thousand characters, and then departed. None knew where he went to in the end.

According to one tradition, Lao Lai Tzu was also a native of the State of Ch'u. He wrote a book in fifteen *p'ien*, setting forth the applications of the teachings of the Taoist school, and was contemporary with Confucius. Lao Tzu probably lived to over a hundred and sixty years of age – some even say over two hundred – as he cultivated the way and was able to live to a great age.

A hundred and twenty nine years after the death of Confucius, it was recorded by a historian that Tan the Historian of Chou had an audience with Duke Hsien of Ch'in during which he said, 'In the first instance, Ch'in and Chou were united, and after being united for five hundred years they separated, but seventy years after the separation a great feudal lord is going to be born.' Acording to some, Tan was none other than Lao Tzu, but according to others this was not so. The world is unable to know where the truth lay. Lao Tzu was a gentleman who lived in retirement from the world.

The son of Lao Tzu was one by the name of Tsung, who served as general in the army of the state of Wei and was given the fief of Tuan Kan. Tsung's son was Chu, Chu's son was Kung, and Kung's great-great-grandson was Chia. Chia was an official in the time of Emperor Wen of the Han Dynasty. His son Chieh was Tutor to Ang, Prince of Chiao Hsi, and as a result made his home in Ch'i.

The followers of Lao Tzu try to belittle the Confucianists, and the Confucianists likewise belittle the followers of Lao Tzu. This may be what is meant when it is said that 'people who follow different ways never have anything helpful to say to one another'.

Li Erh 'does nothing and the people are transformed of their own accord'; 'remains limpid and still and the people are rectified of themselves.'

In the biography of Confucius in the same work, there is another version of his meeting with Lao Tzu:

Nan-kung Ching-shu of Lu said to the king of Lu, 'May your servant be granted permission to go to Chou with Confucius.' The king of Lu gave him a carriage and two horses, together with one servant, and he went [with Confucius] to Chou to ask about the rites. It was probably then that they met Lao Tzu.

When they departed, Lao Tzu saw them off and said, 'I have heard that men of wealth and rank make gifts of money while benevolent men make gifts of words. I have not been able to win either wealth or rank, but I have been undeservedly accorded the name of a benevolent man. These words are my parting gift: "There are men with clever and penetrating minds who are never far from death. This is because they are fond of criticizing others. There are men of wide learning and great eloquence who put themselves in peril. This is because they expose the evil deeds of others. Neither a son nor a subject should look upon his person as his own."'

When Ssu-ma Ch'ien came to write the biography of Lao Tzu, he found so few facts that all he could do was to collect together traditions about the man current in his time. He had difficulty even with Lao Tzu's identity. He explicitly suggests that he was probably the same person as Tan the Historian, though the latter lived more than a century after the death of Confucius. He also implied that there was a possibility that Lao Tzu was Lao Lai Tzu because the latter was also a native of

Ch'u and the author of a Taoist work. Finally, he identifies Lao Tzu as the father of one Tuan-kan Tsung whose descendants were still living in his own time. He expresses his own doubts and misgivings when he says, 'Lao Tzu probably lived to over a hundred and sixty years of age – some even say over two hundred – as he cultivated the way and was able to live to a great age.' He is half-hearted in his identification of Lao Tzu with Tan the Historian as he adds, 'The world is unable to know where the truth lay.' When he goes on to say, 'Lao Tzu was a gentleman who lived in retirement from the world,' he is tacitly offering an explanation for the lack of reliable information in this biography.

Apart from the statement that Lao Tzu's name was Tan and that his native state was Ch'u, there are only two purported facts in the whole biography. The first is the meeting between Lao Tzu and Confucius at which Confucius asked to be instructed in the rites. The second is Lao Tzu's westward journey through the Pass and the writing of a book at the request of the Keeper of the Pass.

Neither of these two purported facts is recorded in any extant work whose date is indubitably early. In my view both traditions did not become widely known or accepted until the period between 280 and 240 B.C., and there are no strong reasons to believe that they were founded on fact. In all probability Lao Tzu was not a historical figure at all. Once we cease to look at Lao Tzu as a historical personage and the *Lao tzu* as written by him, we begin to see certain features concerning both which point to a more reasonable view.

At a very early stage Confucius came to be known as a sage and naturally stories came to be told about him some of which no doubt originated from hostile circles. Of these there was a particular genre which was popular. This consists of stories about Confucius's encounters with hermits who made fun of him. The Lao Tzu story is only one such story and Lao Tzu was only one among a number of such hermits. Since such stories cannot be taken seriously as historical evidence, we have no reason to believe that Lao Tzu was a real person.

Moreover, in the period covering the second half of the fourth and the first half of the third century B.C. there were at least two works with titles which mean 'elder' and 'old man of mature wisdom'. It cannot be accidental that 'Lao Tzu' also has the meaning of 'old man'. There seems to be a genre of literature in this period to which such titles were given. This is probably because these works consist of sayings which embody a kind of wisdom that is associated with old age. There is no reason to suppose that the titles imply that these works were written by individuals. They are best looked upon as anthologies which were compiled from short passages by an editor or a series of editors. Most of these short passages reflect the doctrines of the time but some represent sayings of considerable antiquity.

It is probably because 'Lao Tzu' happened to be the name of one of the hermits in the Confucian stories and also figured as the title of one of these anthologies of wise sayings that the *Lao tzu* alone has survived and is attributed to a man who instructed Confucius in the rites.*

The period in which the *Lao tzu* and other works of the same kind were produced was certainly a golden age of Chinese thought. Schools of thought mushroomed, so much so that

* For a detailed discussion of the *Lao tzu* and its author see Appendices 1 and 2.

they are often referred to as 'the hundred schools'. Scholars and philosophers who could lay claim to any originality in ideas won preferment as well as prestige. This can be seen from the gathering of brilliant minds at Chi Hsia under the patronage of King Wei (356–320 B.C.) and King Hsüan (319–301 B.C.) of the state of Ch'i. As we shall see, in the *Lao tzu* are to be found many ideas which were associated with one or other of the thinkers of this period.

At this time the schools of thought founded by Confucius, Mo Tzu (*fl.* fifth century B.C.) and Yang Chu (*fl.* fourth century B.C.) were the 'prominent schools'. Confucius taught a way of life in which morality occupies a supreme position. Morality is shown to have no connexion whatsoever with self-interest. In fact the demands of morality on a man are categorical. If need be, he has to sacrifice even his life in doing what is right. Confucius's view concerning the actual duties a man has was traditional. A man is born into certain relationships and as a result has certain duties. For instance, he has a duty of loyalty to his lord, a filial duty to his parents, a duty to help his friends, and a duty of common humanity towards his fellow beings. These duties are not of equal stringency. A man's duty to his lord and parents comes before his duty to his friends and fellow human beings. It was Confucius's belief that if everyone lived up to his duties according to his station political order would prevail.

Mo Tzu probably started life as a Confucian but gradually became dissatisfied with some of the tenets of Confucianism. He saw that so long as there were duties varying in stringency there was bound to be discrimination, and conflict could not be completely avoided. It may happen that a man has to do something harmful to another because his duty towards his parents demands it. To prevent this kind of situation from arising, Mo Tzu advocated 'love without discrimination'. A man should love others as himself and also their parents as his own. Mo Tzu also placed greater emphasis than later Confucianists on the doctrine that men of worth should be in authority.

Confucius was also traditional in his attitude to *t'ien* (heaven). Heaven was for him vaguely a divine presence, whose decree it was that men should be moral. Mo Tzu was of a much more religious turn of mind. His conception of heaven was the closest to a personal God that is to be met with in ancient Chinese thought. For him it is the will of heaven that men should love one another without discrimination, and those who fail to do so will be punished. The attitude of Confucius and Mo Tzu to heaven is something we shall have to bear in mind when we come to examine the concept of the *tao* (way) in the *Lao tzu*.

In the case of Yang Chu unfortunately we have no extant work representing his school. According to the writings of other thinkers, some of whom were certainly not sympathetic, Yang Chu advocated a thoroughgoing egoism. We shall have occasion to return to this topic and discuss the precise nature of this egoism. All we need to say here is that it has been suggested that the *Lao tzu* represents a development of the school of Yang Chu. Whether this is altogether justified or not, there certainly are passages in the *Lao tzu* which are best understood in the spirit of Yang Chu's egoism. Such is the background against which the *Lao tzu* is to be understood.

In my view not only is the *Lao tzu* an anthology but even individual chapters are usually made up of shorter passages whose connexion with one another is at best tenuous; to deal then with the thought contained in the work it is necessary to take these short sections rather than the chapters as units, as the work in its present form must have been compiled by a series of editors out of these short sections. It also follows from our view of the work as an anthology that we cannot expect the thought contained in it to be a closely knit system, though the greater part of the work may show some common tendency of thought which can be described as Taoist in the broad sense of the term. Since we cannot expect a high degree of cohesion in the thought, the most sensible way of giving an account of it is to deal with the various key concepts, and to relate them wherever possible, but also to point out inconsistencies when these are obstinately irreconcilable.

A good way of starting this account is to select those concepts that were, from early times, associated with Lao Tzu or the *Lao tzu* (in Chinese there is no linguistic distinction between the two and so it is impossible to know whether it is the man or the book that is referred to when the name 'Lao Tzu' occurs).

From the fact that the school of thought supposed to have been founded by Lao Tzu is known as Taoism (*tao chia*, the school of the way), it can be seen that the *tao* was considered the central concept in the thought contained in the *Lao tzu*. The opening chapter of the *Lao tzu* begins with an important characterization of the *tao*:

> The way that can be spoken of
> Is not the constant way. (1)

In other words, the *tao* that can be described, cited as authority, and praised is not the immutable way. This point is repeated in chapter XXXII:

> The way is for ever nameless (72).

and again in chapter XLI,

> The way conceals itself in being nameless. (92)

There is no name that is applicable to the *tao* because language is totally inadequate for such a purpose. And yet if the *tao* is to be taught at all, some means, no matter how inadequate, must be found to give an idea of what it is like. This is a difficult task, for even the term '*tao*' is not its proper name but a name we use for want of something better, and if we insist on characterizing it in some manner we can only describe it, not altogether appropriately, as 'great' (XXV, 56a).

The difficulty of finding appropriate language to describe the *tao* lies in the fact that although the *tao* is conceived of as that which is responsible for the creation as well as the support of the universe, yet the description the Taoist aimed at was a description in terms of tangible qualities as though the *tao* were a concrete thing.

In chapter XLII, it is said

> The way begets one; one begets two; two begets three; three begets the myriad creatures. (93)

Although here it is said that 'the way begets one', 'the One' is, in fact, very often used as another name for the '*tao*'. Understood in this way, we can see that it is 'the One' or the '*tao*' which is responsible for creating as well as supporting the universe.

> Of old, these came to be in possession of the One:
>   Heaven in virtue of the One is limpid;
>   Earth in virtue of the One is settled;
>   Gods in virtue of the One have their potencies;

The valley in virtue of the One is full;
The myriad creatures in virtue of the One are alive;
Lords and princes in virtue of the One become leaders in
    the empire.
It is the One that makes these what they are. (xxxix, 85)

The point is pressed home by what immediately follows,

Without what makes it limpid heaven might split;
Without what makes it settled earth might sink;
Without what gives them their potencies gods might spend
    themselves;
Without what makes it full the valley might run dry;
Without what keeps them alive the myriad creatures might
    perish;
Without what makes them leaders lords and princes might
    fall. (85a)

If this *tao* which is behind the universe is to be described in
physical terms, this is the result:

Its upper part is not dazzling;
Its lower part is not obscure.
Dimly visible, it cannot be named
And returns to that which is without substance.
This is called the shape that has no shape,
The image that is without substance.
This is called indistinct and shadowy.
Go up to it and you will not see its head;
Follow behind it and you will not see its rear (xiv, 33),

and

As a thing the way is
Shadowy, indistinct.

Indistinct and shadowy,
Yet within it is an image;
Shadowy and indistinct,
Yet within it is a substance.
Dim and dark,
Yet within it is an essence.
This essence is quite genuine
And within it is something that can be tested (XXI, 49),

and

There is a thing confusedly formed,
Born before heaven and earth.
Silent and void
It stands alone and does not change,
Goes round and does not weary. (XXV, 56)

From these passages we can see that the entity called the *tao*
existed before the universe came into being. This, for the author,
is an absolutely indisputable fact. It has an essence which is
genuine, and this genuineness is vouched for by the existence
of the universe which it has produced and continues to sustain.
But beyond this there is nothing we can say about the *tao*. The
difficulty is indicated by saying that it is 'shadowy and indistinct', that it is 'the shape that has no shape, the image that is
without substance'. In fact, even to say that it produced the
universe is misleading. It did not produce the universe in the
same way that a father produces a son.

Deep, it is like the ancestor of the myriad creatures.
(IV, 11)

It images the forefather of God. (IV, 13)

To say that it is 'like' the ancestor of the myriad creatures and that it 'images' the forefather of God is to say that the *tao* produced the universe only in a figurative sense.

For the difficulty of describing the *tao* there is a traditional interpretation which is quite ancient but for which there is no explicit support to be found in the *Lao tzu* itself. This is based on the conception of opposite terms which, as we shall see, play an important part in the thought of the *Lao tzu*. If we use a term to describe the attribute of a thing, there is also a term opposite to it which is suitable for describing the attribute of some other thing. We describe one thing as strong, but also describe another thing as weak. Similarly for the long and the short, the high and the low, and all conceivable pairs of opposites. Now if we wish to characterize the *tao*, we have to use such terms and yet none of them is appropriate, for if the *tao* is responsible for the strong being strong it is no less responsible for the weak being weak. It is argued that in order to be responsible for the strong being strong the *tao* must, in some sense, be itself strong also; and yet it would not be true to describe it as strong because as it is equally responsible for the weak being weak it must, in some sense, be itself weak as well. Thus we can see that no term can be applied to the *tao* because all terms are specific, and the specific, if applied to the *tao*, will impose a limitation on the range of its function. And the *tao* that is limited in its function can no longer serve as the *tao* that sustains the manifold universe.

There is no actual textual support for such an interpretation in the *Lao tzu*, but in all fairness it ought also to be pointed out that there is nothing in the text which is inconsistent with this interpretation either. Whether this is a correct interpretation of the original intention of the *Lao tzu* or not, it is a possible one and has the merit of being interesting philosophically. It forms a striking contrast to the type of metaphysical reasoning in the Western tradition of which Plato is a prominent example. According to Plato, the objects of the sensible world are unreal to the extent that it can be said, at the same time, of any one of them that it is both A and not-A. There is no object in this world, no matter how round, of which we cannot say, at the same time, that it is not round. Therefore it fails to be fully round and so truly real. The Forms, on the other hand, are truly real because it is nonsense to say of the Form of Roundness that it is not round. What in Plato qualifies the Forms for reality is precisely that which would disqualify the *tao* from being the immutable way.

Plato's view results in a plurality of Forms, each distinct in character from all others, while in the Taoist view there can be, and is, only one *tao*. The advantage seems to rest with the Taoist, as Plato was, in the end, unable to rest satisfied with a plurality of Forms and had to bring in the Form of the Good as a unifying principle, though how this unification was contrived is not at all clear. Again, Plato's insistence that of anything real we must be able to make a statement to the exclusion of its contradictory seems to stem from his assumption that the totally real must be totally knowable. Here once more the Taoist takes the opposite position and looks upon the *tao* as unknowable. As before, the advantage seems to rest with the Taoist. There is no reason for us to assume that the totally real is totally knowable, particularly when the real is thought of as transcendent. The only drawback in saying that the real is unknowable is that it follows from this that the truth must also be ineffable. And this the Taoist is quite prepared to accept.

There may be some doubt whether the interpretation just set out was the one intended in the *Lao tzu*, but there is no doubt that in the *Lao tzu* opposite terms are not treated as equally inadequate in the description of the *tao*. If we take pairs of opposite terms like Something and Nothing, the high and the low, the long and the short, and so on, we can have two classes each comprising one of the two terms in each pair. We can call Something, the high, and the long the higher terms, and Nothing, the low, and the short, the lower terms. It is clear that in the *Lao tzu* the lower terms are thought of as far more useful or, at least, far less misleading as descriptions of the *tao*. For instance, Nothing is often used to indicate the *tao*,

> The myriad creatures in the world are born from Something, and Something from Nothing. (XL, 89)

We can easily understand why lower terms are preferred, for these terms are very often expressed in a negative form, and negative terms have not the same limiting function that positive terms have, and, as we have seen, it is the limiting function that makes specific terms unfit for describing the *tao*.

Besides Nothing, there are other lower terms which are important in the *Lao tzu*, but we have to return to them later on. For the time being, it is the use of Nothing as an indication of the nature of the *tao* that interests us, for this is part and parcel of the difference between the Taoist view and the philosophical views we find in the West.

In the Western tradition, up to the beginning of the present century at least, it has generally been assumed that only what exists can be real, so much so that when, at one time, universals were denied existence, an *ad hoc* subsistence had to be invented to give them reality. With the Taoist, however, whatever has existence cannot be real, for whatever exists also suffers from the limitations of the specific. Hence it is thought far less misleading to say of the *tao* that it is like Nothing, though, strictly speaking, the *tao* can be no more like Nothing than it is like Something.

The conception of the *tao* as the creator of the universe is interesting, because, as far as we know, this was an innovation of the Warring States period, and the *Lao tzu* is one of the works where it is to be found. Traditionally, the role of creator belonged to heaven (*t'ien*). This was so from the earliest times. Heaven was the term used in the earliest extant works, the *Book of Odes* and the *Book of History*. It is the term used in the *Analects of Confucius* and the *Mo tzu*, and continued to be used in the *Mencius* and even in the *Hsün tzu*, where, under the influence of Taoist thought, the term had undergone a significant change in meaning. What is interesting is that even in the *Chuang tzu* side by side with the *tao* heaven continued to be a key term. This can be seen from the remark in the *Hsün tzu* (chapter 21) that Chuang Tzu was prevented from realizing the significance of man because of his obsession with the significance of heaven, and this is borne out by the impression one gets in reading the *Chuang tzu*, where heaven is certainly one of the most important concepts, if not the most important.

In these works where the concept of heaven remains central, the term *tao* is always used in the sense of 'the way *of* something', even when it is used without qualifications. In relation to heaven it means the way that heaven follows, and in relation to man it means the way that he ought to follow, whether it be in the leading of his own life or in the government of the state.

In the *Lao tzu*, the *tao* is no longer 'the way of something', but a completely independent entity, and replaces heaven in all its functions. But the *tao* is also the way followed by the inanimate universe as well as by man. As a result, in reading the *Lao tzu* one sometimes gets the feeling that the line is blurred between the *tao* as an entity and the *tao* as an abstract principle which is followed. These two are confused because they share in common the characteristic of transcending the senses. This is a confusion not unlike the one mentioned in chapter XIV:

> What cannot be seen is called evanescent;
> What cannot be heard is called rarefied;
> What cannot be touched is called minute.
> These three cannot be fathomed
> And so they are confused and looked upon as one. (32, 32a)

Since in the *Lao tzu* the term *tao* has, to all intents and purposes, replaced heaven, it is curious to note that the phrase 'the way of heaven' occurs a number of times. In some cases at least, the use of this phrase seems to indicate that the passage belongs to a somewhat different, and most probably earlier, tradition. Apart from two uses in chapters IX and XLVII which are not typical, the phrase occurs only in the last ten chapters, in some of which the ideas contained seem to be contrary to the view taken of the *tao* in the *Lao tzu* generally. In chapter LXXVII we find

> Is not the way of heaven like the stretching of a bow?
> The high it presses down,
> The low it lifts up;
> The excessive it takes from,
> The deficient it gives to. (184)

It is the way of heaven to take from what has in excess in order to make good what is deficient. (184a)

Then in chapter LXXIX,

It is the way of heaven to show no favouritism.
It is for ever on the side of the good man. (192)

In these passages heaven is conceived of as taking an active hand in redressing the iniquities of this world. It is always on the side of the good and the oppressed. This runs contrary to the view of the *tao* generally to be found in the book as something non-personal and amoral.

In replacing the concept of heaven by that of the *tao* although the *Lao tzu* sets itself apart from most ancient works, including to some extent even the *Chuang tzu*, it is by no means unique. In this respect it shows a certain affinity with a group of chapters (12, 36 to 38, and 49) in the *Kuan tzu*, another work, probably of the same period, which is also an anthology of early writings. These chapters have, in recent years, been considered by some scholars as representing the teachings of the school of Sung K'eng and Yin Wen. Sung K'eng is certainly mentioned both in the *Mencius* and the *Hsün tzu*, and is probably the same as the Sung Jung Tzu mentioned in the *Chuang tzu*. There is no doubt that in his strong opposition to war and in his attempt to persuade people that they do not, in fact, desire much, he was very close to the Mohist school. Yet in the bibliographical chapter of the *Han shu* (*History of the Western Han Dynasty*) by Pan Ku (A.D. 32–92), the comment on Sung K'eng is that he advocated views of Huang and Lao, in other words, Taoist views. This seems to be an indication that there was some connexion between the early Taoist schools and the later Mohists.

Although in the *Lao tzu* the *tao* which replaces heaven has ceased to be an intelligence and to be moral, nevertheless, the *Lao tzu* continued in the tradition that man should model his behaviour on heaven, only here he is urged to model himself on the *tao*. In order to do this, we must first find out how the *tao* functions. Although the *tao* is said to leave nothing undone by resorting to no action, there are indications of how it works.

> Turning back is how the way moves;
> Weakness is the means the way employs. (XL, 88)

This sums up the way the *tao* functions. That 'weakness' and other kindred concepts are important in the *Lao tzu* can be seen from the way the thought of the *Lao tzu* is summed up in two works. In the *Lü shih ch'un ch'iu* (chüan 17, pt 7) it is said that Lao Tan valued 'the submissive (*jou*)', while in the *Hsün tzu* (chapter 17) it is said that Lao Tzu saw the value of 'the bent' but not that of 'the straight'. The weak, the submissive, the bent, these are the important concepts in the *Lao tzu* because these are the qualities the *tao* exhibits.

The movement of the *tao* is described as 'turning back'. This is usually interpreted as meaning that the *tao* causes all things to undergo a process of cyclic change. What is weak inevitably develops into something strong, but when this process of development reaches its limit, the opposite process of decline sets in and what is strong once again becomes something weak, and decline reaches its lowest limit only to give way once more to development. Thus there is an endless cycle of development and decline.

There is a further theory concerning the submissive and the weak which is equally prominent in the *Lao tzu*. The submissive and the weak overcome the hard and the strong. Again this is usually given a cyclic interpretation which links up with that of the theory of change. The weak overcomes the strong and in so doing it becomes strong itself and so falls victim in turn to the weak.

The whole interpretation seems reasonable enough at first sight, but as soon as we look more carefully into the value of the submissive and the weak we become aware of certain difficulties. The precept in the *Lao tzu* is that we should 'hold fast to the submissive'. But is the precept tenable if the cyclic interpretation is correct? If we are exhorted to hold fast to the submissive because in the conflict between the hard and the submissive it is the latter that emerges triumphant, is not this triumph short-lived if the submissive becomes hard in the hour of its triumph? This, if true, would make it impossible to put the precept into practice. Moreover, if change is cyclic and a thing that reaches the limit in one direction will revert to the opposite direction, then the precept is both useless and impracticable. It is useless, if both development and decline are inevitable, since the purpose is in the first instance to avoid decline; and impracticable, if it advocates that we should remain stationary in a world of inexorable and incessant change. As this precept of holding fast to the submissive seems central to the teachings in the *Lao tzu*, it is the cyclic interpretation that has to be given up.

It is necessary then to re-interpret both the process of change and the nature of the victory the submissive gains over the hard. First, in the line

Turning back is how the way moves,

we notice that the term used is 'turning back'. To turn back is 'to return to one's roots', and one's roots are of course the submissive and the weak. All that is said is that a thing, once it has reached the limits of development, will return to its roots, i.e. will decline. This is inevitable. Nothing is said about development being equally inevitable once one has returned to one's roots. In other words, it is never said that the process of change is cyclic. In fact, not only is development not inevitable, it is a slow and gradual process, every step of which has to be sustained by deliberate effort. Development and decline are totally different in nature. Development is slow and gradual; decline is quick and abrupt. Development can only be achieved by deliberate effort; decline comes about naturally and inexorably. Rather than a merry-go-round, the process of change is like a children's slide. One climbs laboriously to the top, but once over the edge the downward movement is quick, abrupt, inevitable, and complete. This makes it not only possible, but also useful, to follow the precept of holding fast to the submissive. One can follow the precept by refusing to make the effort necessary for development and in unusual circumstances by making a positive effort to defeat such development. A poor man can remain poor simply by not making the effort to acquire wealth, but should he be left, against his will, a large legacy by a non-Taoist uncle, he can still stubbornly hold on to his poverty by giving the money away.

The point of holding fast to the submissive is to avoid the fall should one become hard, for in a fall, whether from wealth or from power, one tends – at least in the turbulent times of the Warring States period – to lose one's life into the bargain.

This is the reason for advocating that one should both 'know contentment' and 'know when to stop'.

> Know contentment
> And you will suffer no disgrace;
> Know when to stop
> And you will meet with no danger.
> You can then endure. (XLIV, 100)

Again, in chapter XXXIII,

> He who knows contentment is rich. (75)

This point is even more forcefully put in chapter XLVI:

> There is no crime greater than having too many desires;
> There is no disaster greater than not being content;
> There is no misfortune greater than being covetous. (105)

Although development is an uphill climb which needs deliberate effort to sustain it at every step, the impulse to such effort is great and universally present in man. Man is egged on by desire and covetousness to be ever wanting greater gratification, so it is necessary to counter his natural tendencies by the lessons of 'knowing contentment' and 'knowing when to stop'. Only when a man realizes that he has enough can he learn not to aim at winning greater wealth and more exalted rank, the ceaseless pursuit of which will end only in disaster.

There is still the victory of the submissive and the weak over the hard and the strong to be explained in a way consistent with the precept of holding fast to the submissive. The explanation lies in the fact that, in achieving victory over the hard and the strong, the submissive and the weak do not become their opposites. In order to understand this, we must bear in mind the fact that in the *Lao tzu* a term is often used in two senses, the ordinary and the Taoist. 'Victory' is such a term. In the ordinary sense of the word, it is the strong that gains 'victory' over the weak. In this sense, victory cannot be guaranteed indefinitely, as however strong a thing is, it is inevitable that one day it will meet with more than its match. The Taoist sense of the word 'victory', in contrast, is rather paradoxical. The weak does not contend, and so no one in the world can pick a quarrel with it. If one never contends, this at least ensures that one never suffers defeat. One may even wear down the resistance of one's stronger opporent by this passive weapon of non-contention, or at least wait for him to meet with defeat at the hands of someone stronger. It is in this sense that the submissive and the weak gain 'victory' over the hard and the strong.

> To hold fast to the submissive is called strength. (LII, 119)

'The virtue of non-contention' enables a man to 'defeat his enemy without joining issue' (LXVIII, 166 and 166a). There are many passages in praise of this 'virtue of non-contention'.

> It is because he does not contend that no one in the empire is in a position to contend with him. (XXII, 50c; also LXVI, 162)

> It is because it does not contend that it is never at fault. (VIII, 22)

As we have seen, the value of the Taoist precept of holding fast to the submissive lies in its usefulness as a means to survival. This being the case, we may feel that the *Lao tzu* attaches an undue importance to survival. This feeling shows that we have not succeeded in understanding the environment that produced the hopes and fears which were crystallized into such a precept. The centuries in which the *Lao tʒu* was produced were certainly turbulent times. China was divided into a number of states, to all intents and purposes autonomous, constantly engaged in wars of increasing scope and ferocity with one another. For the common man survival was a real and pressing problem. It was to the solution of this problem of survival that much of the wisdom of the *Lao tʒu* is directed. To the Taoist,

He who lives out his days has had a long life. (XXXIII, 75)

Unless one can feel some sympathy for the aspirations of men who could never be sure from one day to another whether they would manage to stay alive, the precept will strike one as singularly negative and pessimistic.

There are a number of pacifist passages in the *Lao tʒu* where one can detect a passionate concern for the lot of the common man in times of war.

Arms are instruments of ill-omen . . . When great numbers of people are killed, one should weep over them with sorrow. When victorious in war, one should observe the rites of mourning. (XXXI, 71)

Again,

Where troops have encamped
There will brambles grow;
In the wake of a mighty army
Bad harvests follow without fail. (XXX, 69a)

The use of arms is a desperate remedy, and one should resort to it 'only when there is no choice' (XXX, 69b), and 'of two sides raising arms against each other, it is the one that is sorrow-stricken that wins' (LXIX, 169).

There is also a solemn warning to the rulers that if the people are relentlessly oppressed there comes a point when they might not even wish to survive. When that happens the ruler will find himself robbed of the only effective tool of oppression.

> When the people are not afraid of death, wherefore frighten them with death? (LXXIV, 180)

Moreover, if the time ever comes when people no longer fear death, then something terrible will happen, and it will not be the people alone who will suffer. The ruler will perish with them:

> When the people lack a proper sense of awe, then some awful visitation will descend upon them. (LXXII, 174)

In its concern for the common man, the *Lao tzu* shows some similarities to the works of Hobbes, who, in his own way, was equally preoccupied with the problem of survival, as can be seen from the opening remark in his autobiography that his mother gave birth to twins, himself and fear. But if the motive of fear is the same, the solution offered is totally different. In his *Leviathan*, Hobbes sets out to devise a political system that would offer security for the common man, while in the *Lao tzu* there are only precepts to help the common man to survive in the perilous situation in which he finds himself. Perhaps this is because, for the Taoist, the only hope of a world offering security to the common man lies in the conversion of some ruler to Taoism, and he is not over-sanguine about the chances of this being realized. At any rate, it may be a long time before this can happen and it is necessary for the common man to have precepts to live by which will enable him to survive in the meantime. These precepts are based on the value of meekness to survival. That even meekness is not an infallible means was a lesson only to be found in parts of the *Chuang tzu*.

Almost all ancient Chinese thinkers were concerned with the way one should lead one's life, and this was never confined to conduct in the personal sense, but covered the art of government as well. Politics and ethics, for the Chinese as for the ancient Greeks, were two aspects of the same thing, and this the Chinese thinkers called the *tao*. One who has the *tao* will, in the words of the *T'ien hsia* chapter of the *Chuang tzu*, be 'inwardly a sage and outwardly a true king'. This was the general outlook of the period, and the *Lao tzu* was no exception. This can be seen even from one simple fact. The term 'sage (*sheng jen*)' occurs more than twenty times in the *Lao tzu* and, with only a few exceptions, refers always to a ruler who understands the *tao*.* Besides 'the sage', there are other terms as well that refer to rulers, like 'the lord of men' and 'lords and princes'. This shows that the *Lao tzu* is, through and through, a work on the art of government.

The sage is first and foremost a man who understands the *tao*, and if he happens also to be a ruler he can apply his understanding of the *tao* to government. The knowledge of the *tao* makes the sage a good ruler because the government of the people should be modelled on the way the myriad creatures in the universe are ruled by the *tao*.

We have seen that the term 'Nothing (*wu*)' is sometimes

---

* The sage in the Taoist sense is to be distinguished from the sage in the conventional sense whose extermination is said to benefit the people a hundredfold (xix, 43).

used for the *tao*, because, if we must characterize the *tao* by one of a pair of opposite terms, the negative is preferable because it is less misleading. It follows that as 'Nothing' is preferable to 'Something' so are other negative terms to their positive opposites. Two of these negative terms are central to the Taoist theory of the function of the ruler. The first is '*wu wei*'; the second is '*wu ming*'. *Wu wei* literally means 'without action', and *wu ming* 'without name'. These terms came to be coined probably because they are phrases in which *wu* ('not to have' and so 'nothing') forms the first element. This does not mean that the connexion between *wu wei* and *wu ming*, on the one hand, and *wu*, on the other, is purely a linguistic one. They are, like *wu*, negative terms. What makes *wu* a suitable term for describing the *tao* makes these terms suitable as well. To say of the *tao* that it acts is to limit its effectiveness, because merely by doing some things, it must, by implication, leave other things undone. To say that it does not act at least leaves it untrammelled: no special relation exists between the *tao* and certain affairs to the exclusion of others.

> The way never acts yet nothing is left undone. (XXXVII, 81)

This passage goes on to say that

> Should lords and princes be able to hold fast to it,
> The myriad creatures will be transformed of their own accord.

This is a clear statement that the ruler should model himself on the *tao* and follow the policy of resorting to no action. The reasons for this policy are never very clearly stated, but some indications are given.

T – B

Whoever takes the empire and wishes to do anything to it I see will have no respite. The empire is a sacred vessel and nothing should be done to it. Whoever does anything to it will ruin it; whoever lays hold of it will lose it. (XXIX, 66)

Again,

Governing a large state is like boiling a small fish. (LX, 138)

In both passages we see that the state or the empire is a delicate thing that can be ruined by the least handling, or a sacred vessel which must not be tampered with. The empire is as much a part of the natural order as the world of inanimate objects and, being part of the natural order, will run smoothly so long as everyone follows his own nature. To think that one can improve on nature by one's petty cleverness is profanity. The natural order is delicately balanced. The least interference on the part of the ruler will upset this balance and lead to disorder.

The ideal state of the Taoist is one in which the people are innocent of knowledge and free from desire. By 'desire' here is not meant desire for basic necessities like food and clothing. For the Taoist, food is for satisfying hunger and clothes for warding off the cold. Anything going beyond these aims would be luxuries. Food is a basic need; delicacies are objects of desire. Clothes are a basic need; fineries are objects of desire. But we must not think that it is beauty alone that excites desire. Goodness, also, excites desire. Government necessarily involves the setting up of values. Certain modes of conduct are considered good and desirable, and merit, besides being desirable in itself, brings with it rewards which are coveted either for themselves or as emblems of privilege. These are all the results of the interfering acts of the ruler, and he must realize this and avoid such action.

> Not to honour men of worth will keep the people from contention; not to value goods which are hard to come by will keep them from theft; not to display what is desirable will keep them from being unsettled of mind. (III, 8)

The opening phrase in this passage is a direct attack on the doctrine of 'honouring men of worth' which was a basic tenet in the Mohist theory of government but which was also advocated by later Confucianists.

Desire in a sense is secondary to knowledge on which it is dependent. It is through the knowledge of what is desirable that desire is excited. It is also through knowledge that new objects of desire are devised. It is for this reason that knowledge and the clever come in for constant stricture. If the Taoist philosopher could have visited our society, there is no doubt that he would have considered popular education and mass advertising the twin banes of modern life. The one causes the people to fall from their original state of innocent ignorance; the other creates new desires for objects no one would have missed if they had not been invented.

The task of the ruler, then, is to avoid doing anything, so that the people will not gain new knowledge and acquire fresh desires.

> Of old those who excelled in the pursuit of the way did not use it to enlighten the people but to hoodwink them. The reason why the people are difficult to govern is that they are too clever. (LXV, 157)

Again,

> In governing the people, the sage empties their minds but fills
> their bellies, weakens their wills but strengthens their bones.
> He always keeps them innocent of knowledge and free from
> desire, and ensures that the clever never dare to act. (III, 9)

Again,

> The sage in his attempt to distract the mind of the empire seeks
> urgently to muddle it. The people all have something to occupy
> their eyes and ears, and the sage treats them all like children.
> (XLIX, 112)

The aim of the sage is to keep the people in a childlike state
where there is no knowledge and so no desire beyond the
immediate objects of the senses.

In connexion with the freedom from desire, it is necessary to
say something about the 'uncarved block'. There may be
other implications of this symbol, but there are two features
which stand out prominently.

Firstly, the uncarved block is in a state as yet untouched by
the artificial interference of human ingenuity and so is a symbol
for the original state of man before desire is produced in him by
artificial means. By holding firmly to the principle of non-action
exhibited by the *tao*, the ruler will be able to transform the
people, but

> After they are transformed, should desire raise its head,
> I shall press it down with the weight of the nameless un-
>   carved block.
> The nameless uncarved block
> Is but freedom from desire,

36

> And if I cease to desire and remain still,
> The empire will be at peace of its own accord. (XXXVII, 81)

Again, the sage says

> I am free from desire and the people of themselves become
> simple like the uncarved block. (LVII, 133)

Even after the people are transformed, the sage has to be constantly on the look-out in case 'desire should raise its head', and the way to keep the people in a simple state like the uncarved block is to be himself free from desire.

Secondly, the uncarved block is also said to be 'nameless'. This, as we have said, is one of the important attributes of the ruler. But the meaning of the term 'nameless' deserves careful examination, because it has a further meaning besides the obvious one of 'not being known'.

> When the uncarved block shatters it becomes vessels. The sage
> makes use of these and becomes the lord over the officials.
> (XXVIII, 64)

Now 'vessel' is a term used, from early times, to denote a specialist. In the *Analects of Confucius*, for instance, we find the saying, 'A gentleman is no vessel' (2. 12), meaning that the concern of the gentleman is the art of government and not the knowledge of a specialist. The nameless uncarved block is nameless because it has not shattered and become vessels. Hence it is the symbol of the ruler.

> Though the uncarved block is small
> No one in the world dare claim its allegiance. (XXXII, 72)

We may recall that no name is adequate as a description for the *tao* because a name is always the name of a specific thing and so will limit the function of the *tao*. Similarly, the ruler is nameless because he is no specialist and only specialists can be named. It is in virtue of his knowledge of the *tao* that the ruler is able to rule over his officials who, being specialists, can only be entrusted with departmental duties.

The obvious lesson the ruler can learn from the *tao* is this. Being nameless, it is self-effacing. In relation to the myriad creatures,

> It gives them life yet claims no possession;
> It benefits them yet exacts no gratitude;
> It is the steward yet exercises no authority. (LI, 116)

The ruler must, likewise, be self-effacing in his relation to the people.

> The sage benefits them yet exacts no gratitude,
> Accomplishes his task yet lays claim to no merit.
> (LXXVII, 185)

In fact,

> The best of all rulers is but a shadowy presence to his subjects,

and

> When his task is accomplished and his work done
> The people all say 'It happened to us naturally'.
> (XCII, 39, 41)

In connexion with the subject of the art of government the *Lao tzu* is often charged with advocating the use of 'scheming methods (*yin mou*)'. This is obviously based on the opening passage in chapter XXXVI:

> If you would have a thing shrink,
> You must first stretch it;

> If you would have a thing weakened,
> You must first strengthen it;
> If you would take from a thing,
> You must first give to it. (79)

The interpretation of this passage is certainly not open to question, but it is another matter whether this can justifiably be extended to other passages, such as:

> The sage puts his own person last and it comes first,
> Treats it as extraneous to himself and it is preserved.
> Is it not because he is without thought of self that he is able to
> accomplish his private ends? (VII, 19, 19a)

and

> Desiring to rule over the people,
> One must, in one's words, humble oneself before them;
> And, desiring to lead the people,
> One must, in one's person, follow behind them. (LXVI, 160)

These passages seem to support the charge only so long as we have the preconceived notion that the *Lao tzu* advocates the use of 'scheming methods'. But if we approach them with an open mind, we begin to see that there need not be anything sinister in what is said, which is no more than this. Even if a ruler were to aim at realizing his own ends he can only hope to succeed by pursuing the ends of the people. If he values his own person he can only serve its best interest by treating it as extraneous to himself. What is here said about the realization of the ruler's private ends is reminiscent of what is sometimes said about the pursuit of happiness. A man can achieve his own happiness only by pursuing the happiness of others, because it is only by forgetting about his own happiness that he can become happy. This has never been looked upon as a sinister theory. No more need be the theory in the *Lao tzu*. It is not said in the passages quoted that the ruler should pursue his own ends at the expense of the people. This would indeed be a vicious view, but that is precisely what is said here, by implication, not to be possible, even if one were to grant that it is desirable.

In fact true selfishness is a very rare thing and when it is found in a man it makes him eminently suitable to be a ruler. A truly selfish man is one who would not allow excessive indulgence in the good things in life to harm his body. Such a person is unlikely to take advantage of the people for the sake of gratifying his own desires were he made ruler. Hence it is said,

> He who values his body more than dominion over the empire can be entrusted with the empire. He who loves his body more than dominion over the empire can be given the custody of the empire. (XIII, 31)

This probably represented the view of the school of Yang Chu. In a conversation between Yang Chu and Ch'in Ku-li recorded in the *Yang chu* chapter of the *Lieh tzu*, Yang Chu is said to have remarked, 'A man of old would not have given a hair even if he could have benefited the empire by doing so, but neither would he have accepted the empire were it offered to him for his exclusive enjoyment.' The second half of the statement is a fair representation of Yang Chu's position, but the first half is a distortion similar to the statement by Mencius that 'Yang Tzu chose egoism and even if he could have benefited the empire by pulling out one hair he would not have done so' (7A. 26). It has been pointed out by Dr A. C. Graham* that the true posi-

* 'The dialogue between Yang Chu and Chyntzyy', *Bulletin of the School of Oriental and African Studies*, vol. XXII (1959), pp. 291-9.

tion of Yang Chu was that even if he could have *gained* the empire by losing one hair he would have refused to do so. This is surely right, and Yang Chu's ideal was the truly selfish man who would neither harm himself to the least degree in order to gain the empire nor use the empire for his own enjoyment lest such indulgence should be detrimental to his body. Such a man, according to the *Lao tzu*, is eminently suited to rule over the empire.

As passages which seem to support the charge against *Lao tzu* are capable of a different interpretation, we are left with only section 79 as sole grounds for it, and this happens to be a passage which has close parallels which the *Han fei tzu*, the *Chan kuo ts'e*, and the *Lü shih ch'un ch'iu* all attribute to works other than the *Lao tzu*. It seems reasonable to assume that it is a saying of considerable antiquity which belonged to a tradition somewhat different from that to which the greater part of the *Lao tzu* belongs.

From what we have said about the *Lao tzu* it can be seen that the central idea is quite simple and has a direct bearing on life. In life, whether in its ethical or political aspect, we should model ourselves on the *tao*. The supreme goal for the common man as well as for the ruler is survival, and the means to this goal is simply to hold fast to the submissive. No wonder it is said,

> My words are very easy to understand and very easy to put into practice. (LXX, 170)

If few can understand them it is because

> Straightforward words
> Seem paradoxical, (LXXVIII, 189)

and

> When the worst student hears about the way
> He laughs out loud. (XLI, 90)

That no one can put into practice the advice contained in the words is because it is against the grain of human nature in its degenerate form to act in accordance with it.

There are certain ideas which we have, so far, not touched on in our account and to these we must turn our attention. As the work is known as the *Tao te ching*, it must seem strange that we have not said anything about the term '*te*'. *Te* means 'virtue', and seems to be related to its homophone meaning 'to get'. In its Taoist usage, *te* refers to the virtue of a thing (which is what it 'gets' from the *tao*). In other words, *te* is the nature of a thing, because it is in virtue of its *te* that a thing is what it is. But in the *Lao tzu* the term is not a particularly important one and is often used in its more conventional senses.

There are two passages which seem to go against the general tenor of the work. The first is the passage in chapter XIII in which it is said,

> The reason I have great trouble is that I have a body. When I no longer have a body, what trouble have I? (30a)

This is enlightenment indeed, but does not fit well into the *Lao tzu* where survival is assumed, without question, to be the supreme goal in life.

The second is the passage in chapter II,

> Thus Something and Nothing produce each other;
> The difficult and the easy complement each other;
> The long and the short off-set each other;

> The high and the low incline towards each other;
> Note and sound harmonize with each other;
> Before and after follow each other. (5)

The point here made is that opposite terms are relative. Take away the high, and there will no longer be the low. This line of thought, pushed to its logical conclusion, is capable of destroying the distinction between opposites. When the distinction between life and death is abolished, death is no longer something to be feared. This again goes against the general tendency in the *Lao tzu* where not only is survival a supreme value but the distinction between opposites is basic. Take away this basis, and you render superfluous almost everything that is said in the book. Both these passages fit in much better with the kind of Taoist thought to be found in the most important parts of the *Chuang tzu* where the problem that is the main concern of the *Lao tzu* is solved by cutting the Gordian knot.

There are certain ways of interpreting the thought of the *Lao tzu* which are very common but which do not seem to me to be well founded. Both in China and in the West, there have been attempts to put undue emphasis on the mysterious elements in the *Lao tzu*. So far we have seen only a rather down-to-earth philosophy aimed at the mundane purpose of personal survival and political order. There are a few passages which form the basis of this emphasis on the mysterious. These are of two kinds: the first concerns the origin of the universe; the second concerns certain practices of the individual. In the first, we often find the term 'the mother of the myriad creatures', but the term which lends itself most easily to such a purpose is 'the mysterious female', which occurs in chapter VI,

The spirit of the valley never dies.
This is called the mysterious female.
The gateway of the mysterious female
Is called the root of heaven and earth.
Dimly visible, it seems as if it were there,
Yet use will never drain it. (17)

It is possible, however, to take this as a piece of cosmogony. Just as living creatures are born from the womb of the mother, so is the universe born from the womb of 'the mysterious female'. It is a remote possibility that the language used here is an echo of some primitive creation myth. But even if that were the case, the language in the *Lao tzu* has no longer any mythical significance, as can be seen from the description of 'the mysterious female' as 'dimly visible' and seemingly there. It is no more than a picturesque way of describing how the universe came to be, and an expression of wonder at the inexhaustible nature of this creative process. The comparison of the creative processes of nature with the union of male and female is not limited to this passage. Further examples are,

Heaven and earth will unite and sweet dew will fall,
(XXXII, 72)

and

The myriad creatures carry on their backs the *yin* and embrace in their arms the *yang*, and are the blending of the generative forces of the two. (XLII, 94)

It seems hardly justifiable to take such passages and interpret the whole work in the light of them.

The second type of passage deals with practices of the individual and has 'the new born babe' as a symbol.

44

One who possesses virtue in abundance is comparable to a
new born babe. (LV, 125)

Again,

> If you are a ravine to the empire,
> Then the constant virtue will not desert you
> And you will again return to being a babe. (XXVIII, 63)

What is it, we may ask, in a baby that makes it a suitable symbol
for a state so desirable in the eyes of the Taoist? It is its supple-
ness.

> Its bones are weak and its sinews supple yet its hold is
> firm. (LV, 125)

We have seen that *jou* (supple, pliant, submissive) is looked
upon as the quality resembling most closely that of the *tao*,
and because of this,

> A man is supple and weak when living, but hard and stiff when
> dead. Grass and trees are pliant and fragile when living, but
> dried and shrivelled when dead. Thus the hard and the strong
> are the comrades of death; the supple and the weak are the
> comrades of life. (LXXVI, 182)

It may be noted, in passing, that the insight thus gained
into the nature of things is an intuitive one. The Taoist sees
that water is submissive and weak yet it can wear down the
hardest of things, that the baby is supple and weak yet no one
wishes to harm it, that the female is meek and submissive yet
she is able to get the better of the male, that the body is supple
when alive and rigid when dead, and from these isolated observa-
tions he gains the intuitive insight that in the nature of the
universe it is the submissive that survives and triumphs in the

end. Once this intuition is gained, further observation is unnecessary and serves only to confuse.

> Without stirring abroad
> One can know the whole world;
> Without looking out of the window
> One can see the way of heaven.
> The further one goes
> The less one knows. (XLVII, 106)

About the new born babe there is one passage which seems to show a different point of view.

> In concentrating your breath can you become as supple
> As a babe? (X, 24)

It is possible that the concentrating of the breath implies some sort of breathing exercise or perhaps even yogic practice. But again this is an isolated passage in the *Lao tzu*, and what may be even more significant is that this passage has parallels in chapter 37 of the *Kuan tzu* and chapter 23 of the *Chuang tzu*, and in the latter work the passage occurs in a story concerning Lao Tzu and is attributed by him to a book on the safeguarding of life (*Wei sheng chih ching*). It is therefore possible that the passage belongs properly to a school which was given to practices thought to be conducive to the prolonging of life. In the *Lao tzu* the aim is rather to avoid an untimely death through the adoption of submissiveness as a principle of conduct than the prolonging of life beyond its natural limit by artificial practices popular with the seekers after immortality.

There is another common assumption that needs examination. Ever since Wang Pi (A.D. 226–49) who wrote a commentary on the *Book of Changes* as well as on the *Lao tzu*, there has been no

46

lack of interpreters who found affinity between the two works. But it seems to me that this assumption is mistaken. Elsewhere* I have argued that the interpretation of the theory of change as cyclic is more appropriate to the *Book of Changes* than to the *Lao tzu*. Here I wish only to call attention to the *yin* and the *yang*, the central concepts in the *Book of Changes* and the basis for the process of cyclic change. In the *Lao tzu*, the *yin* and the *yang* appear only once, in section 94 which has been quoted above. This is perhaps related to another passage,

> When carrying on your head your perplexed bodily soul
>   can you embrace in your arms the One
> And not let go? (x, 24)

If this is so, then section 94 probably belongs to the same group as section 24, which, as we have just seen, represents the school given to practices conducive to the prolonging of life, a tradition quite different from that of the main part of the *Lao tzu*. This may be speculation, but the fact remains that the *yin* and the *yang* appear once and once only in the whole of the *Lao tzu* and there is no reason to suppose that they occupy an important place in the thought of the whole work.

As in our view the *Lao tzu* is an anthology, it is a matter of some interest and importance that we should try to identify in it the views of some of the thinkers of the Warring States period whose works are unfortunately no longer extant.

We have seen for instance that views similar to those of Yang Chu can be found in passages where the ideal ruler is represented as the truly selfish man. We have also seen that in replacing the

* See my article, 'The Treatment of Opposites in *Lao Tzu*', *Bulletin of the School of Oriental and African Studies*, vol. XXI (1958), pp. 344–60.

concept of heaven by that of the *tao*, the *Lao tzu* bears some resemblance to parts of the *Kuan tzu* which, in the opinion of some modern scholars, are the work of the school of Sung K'eng and Yin Wen who figured among the scholars gathered in Chi Hsia in the state of Ch'i.

Again, according to the *Lü shih ch'un ch'iu* (chüan 17, pt 7), the key concept in the teachings of the legendary Kuan Yin (Keeper of the Pass) is 'limpidity'. In the *T'ien hsia* chapter of the *Chuang tzu*, in an account of the thought of Kuan Yin and Lao Tzu, the former is quoted as saying, presumably in connexion with the sage, 'There is nothing inflexible in him, and so things show themselves up clearly. In his movement he is like water; in his stillness he is like a mirror; in his response he is like an echo. Indistinct, he seems shadowy; silent, he seems limpid. . . . He never leads but always follows behind others.' Here, besides 'limpidity', there are other concepts, many of which, like 'water', 'stillness', 'indistinct', 'shadowy', 'to follow and not to lead', are to be found in the *Lao tzu*. As Kuan Yin is so closely associated with the story of the westward journey of Lao Tzu, it is not surprising that so many of the ideas attributed to Kuan Yin are to be found in the *Lao tzu*.

Lieh Tzu, who is as nebulous a figure as Lao Tzu, was said to have advocated 'emptiness (*hsü*)' (*Lü shih ch'un ch'iu*, loc. cit.), and 'emptiness' figures very prominently in the *Lao tzu*, although the term used, except in sections 15 and 37, is *ch'ung* and not *hsü*.

The most fascinating case is Shen Tao (and T'ien P'ien who is invariably mentioned with him) who not only figured at Chi Hsia but, one suspects, was at least as prominent in the

Warring States period as Chuang Tzu or Lao Tzu as representative of what was later called Taoist thought. He is said in the *T'ien hsia* chapter of the *Chuang tzu* to 'discard wisdom', 'to laugh at the empire for honouring men of worth', 'to consider wrong the great sages of the empire'. He is quoted as saying, 'The highest thing we can hope to emulate is the insensate. Men of worth and sages serve no useful purpose, as the clod never strays from the way.' According to the *Hsün tzu* (chapter 17), he was able to see the value of following behind but not the value of taking the lead. It is somewhat surprising that all his views that we have mentioned are to be found somewhere in the *Lao tzu*. His attack on wisdom, men of worth, and sages is identical with the opening lines of chapter XIX,

> Exterminate the sage, discard the wise,
> And the people will benefit a hundredfold, (43)

and the opening words of chapter III,

> Not to honour men of worth will keep the people from contention. (8)

The value of not taking the lead is also to be found in a number of passages some of which we have already quoted in connexion with the refutation of the charge of the use of scheming methods. It is also found in chapter LXVII,

> I have three treasures
> Which I hold and cherish.

> The third is known as not daring to take the lead in the empire.

> Not daring to take the lead in the empire one could afford to be lord over the vessels.

49

> Now ... to forsake the rear for the lead is sure to end in
> death. (164, 164a)

Finally, Shen Tao's insensate clod is singularly like the uncarved block in the *Lao tzu*, the symbol for freedom from
desire.

We have said enough to show that passages are to be
found in the *Lao tzu* which contain key concepts of the various
schools of the Warring States period, but unfortunately we
cannot take our investigations any further in this direction, for
two reasons. Firstly, we know far too little about most of these
early schools whose representative works are no longer extant.
Secondly, from the key concepts associated with these schools
one gets the impression that very often there is more difference
between them in terminology than in substance. Does not
'valuing the submissive', or 'valuing the empty', or 'avoiding
the lead' amount to the same thing? May it not be the case that
some of these schools were very much alike but each had to
put up a different 'slogan' in order to justify the claim to be an
independent school, since in the Warring States period so much
was to be gained by such a claim? If this is so, there is perhaps
much to say for looking upon all the schools represented in the
Lao tzu as coming under the general description of Taoism, as
the historians of the Han certainly did. Whatever the truth of
the matter, with the scanty material at our disposal we cannot
hope to sort out what pertains to the different schools; though
the little we can do reinforces our conviction that the *Lao tzu*
is an anthology in which are to be found passages representing
the views of various schools, including some which flourished
at Chi Hsia in the second half of the fourth and the first half of the

third century B.C. and which shared the general tendency in thought that came to be known as Taoism.

In the translation, the division into chapters in the traditional text has been adhered to, but section numbers have been introduced. These serve to separate existing chapters into parts which, in my view, need not originally have belonged together. This does not mean that in every case these could not, in fact, have formed a continuous whole. If the reader can see a connexion between parts that I have separated, he can simply ignore my section markings. I have used this method in preference to rearrangement of the text which has been attempted by Eastern as well as Western scholars, because I am unable to share their assumptions that the present text is not in the proper order and that there is a proper order which can be restored by rearrangement. Where two passages are possibly independent, I have given them different section numbers, but when a passage is followed by another which serves as further exposition and was probably added by some editor, I have used the same section number but with an added letter after it.

As considerably more than half of the text consists in rhyming passages which are most probably of an earlier date, it seems desirable to separate them from the prose parts. This is done by printing the translation of the rhyming passages in separate lines and with indention. Needless to say, no attempt has been made to translate these passages in verse form.

The text I have followed is that of the standard Wang Pi version. Wherever I have departed from the standard text, I give the variant reading in a note. I have, however, not thought it necessary to give detailed citation of my authority, as the reader who is interested in the matter can easily find this information in a number of excellent works in which variant readings have been collated, for instance Ma Hsü-lun, *Lao tzu ho ku* (1924; reprinted Peking, 1956), Chiang Hsi-ch'ang, *Lao tzu chiao ku* (Shanghai, 1937), and Chu Ch'ien-chih, *Lao tzu chiao shih* (Shanghai, 1958). Of these Chiang's work is still the most convenient for reference.

D.C.L.

LAO TZU

BOOK ONE

I

1 The way that can be spoken of
  Is not the constant way;
  The name that can be named
  Is not the constant name.

2 The nameless was the beginning of heaven and
    earth;
  The named was the mother of the myriad creatures.

3 Hence always rid yourself of desires in order to
    observe its* secrets;
  But always allow yourself to have desires in order
    to observe its manifestations.[1]†

3a These two are the same
  But diverge in name as they issue forth.
  Being the same they are called mysteries,
  Mystery upon mystery –
  The gateway of the manifold secrets.

---

* In translating from the Chinese it is often impossible to avoid
using the pronouns 'it' and 'they' and their derivatives without
any clear reference, whether these are expressed in the Chinese
or only implied. In the present work 'it' used in this way sometimes refers to 'the way' and 'they' to 'the myriad creatures'.
† Superior arabic figures refer to notes, mainly of a textual
nature, placed at the end of the book.

II

4 The whole world recognizes the beautiful as the beautiful, yet this is only the ugly; the whole world recognizes the good as the good, yet this is only the bad.

5 Thus Something and Nothing produce each other;
The difficult and the easy complement each other;
The long and the short off-set[1] each other;
The high and the low incline towards each other;
Note and sound* harmonize with each other;
Before and after follow each other.†

6 Therefore the sage keeps to the deed that consists in taking no action and practises the teaching that uses no words.

7 The myriad creatures rise from it yet it claims no authority;[2]
It gives them life yet claims no possession;
It benefits them yet exacts no gratitude;
It accomplishes its task yet lays claim to no merit.

7a It is because it lays claim to no merit
That its merit never deserts it.

* The Chinese terms used here are not precise and it is not clear what the intended contrast is. The translation is, therefore, tentative.

† It may seem strange to say that before and after follow each other, but this refers probably to a ring. Any point on a ring is both before and after any other point, depending on the arbitary choice of the starting-point.

III

8 Not to honour men of worth will keep the people from contention; not to value goods which are hard to come by will keep them from theft; not to display what is desirable will keep them from being unsettled of mind.

9 Therefore in governing the people, the sage empties their minds but fills their bellies, weakens their wills but strengthens their bones. He always keeps them innocent of knowledge and free from desire, and ensures that the clever never dare to act.

10 Do that which consists in taking no action, and order will prevail.

IV

11   The way is empty, yet use will not drain*[1] it.
     Deep, it is like the ancestor of the myriad creatures.

12   Blunt the sharpness;
     Untangle the knots;
     Soften the glare;
     Let your wheels move only along old ruts.[2]

13   Darkly visible, it only seems as if it were there.
     I know not whose son it is.
     It images the forefather of God.

* The word in the text meaning 'full' has been emended to one meaning 'empty'. Cf. 'Yet use will never drain it' (17); 'Yet it cannot be exhausted by use' (78); 'Yet use will not drain it' (101).

V

14   Heaven and earth are ruthless, and treat the myriad
     creatures as straw dogs*; the sage is ruthless, and
     treats the people as straw dogs.

15   Is not the space between heaven and earth like a
     bellows?
     It is empty without being exhausted:
     The more it works the more comes out.

16   Much speech leads inevitably to silence.
     Better to hold fast to the void.[1]

---

* In the *T'ien yün* chapter in the *Chuang tzu* it is said that straw
dogs were treated with the greatest deference before they were
used as an offering, only to be discarded and trampled upon as
soon as they had served their purpose.

VI

17   The spirit of the valley never dies.
This is called the mysterious female.
The gateway of the mysterious female
Is called the root of heaven and earth.
Dimly visible, it seems as if it were there,
Yet use will never drain it.

VII

18 Heaven and earth are enduring. The reason why heaven and earth can be enduring is that they do not give themselves life. Hence they are able to be long-lived.

19 Therefore the sage puts his person last and it comes first,

Treats it as extraneous to himself and it is preserved.

19a Is it not because he is without thought of self that he is able to accomplish his private ends?

VIII

20   Highest good is like water. Because water excels in benefiting the myriad creatures without contending with them and settles where none would like to be, it comes close to the way.

21   In a home it is the site that matters;[1]
In quality of mind it is depth that matters;
In an ally it is benevolence that matters;
In speech it is good faith that matters;
In government it is order that matters;
In affairs it is ability that matters;
In action it is timeliness that matters.

22   It is because it does not contend that it is never at fault.*

* In sense and, possibly, in rhyme, this line is continuous with 20.

IX

23   Rather than fill it to the brim by keeping it upright
Better to have stopped in time;[*1]
Hammer it to a point
And the sharpness cannot be preserved for ever;
There may be gold and jade to fill a hall
But there is none who can keep them.
To be overbearing when one has wealth and
    position
Is to bring calamity upon oneself.
To retire when the task is accomplished
Is the way of heaven.

* This refers to a vessel which is said to have been in the temple of Chou (or Lu). It stands in position when empty but overturns when full. The moral is that humility is a necessary virtue, especially for those in high position.

X

24 When carrying on your head[1] your perplexed bodily
soul* can you embrace in your arms the One
And not let go?
In concentrating your breath can you become as
supple
As a babe?
Can you polish your mysterious mirror†
And leave no blemish?
Can you love the people and govern the state
Without resorting to action?[2]
When the gates of heaven‡ open and shut
Are you capable of keeping to the role of the female?[3]
When your discernment penetrates the four quarters
Are you capable of not knowing anything?[4]

25 It gives them life and rears them.

26 It gives them life yet claims no possession;
It benefits them yet exacts no gratitude;
It is the steward yet exercises no authority.
Such is called the mysterious virtue.

* Man has two souls, the *p'o* which is the soul of the body and
the *hun* which is the soul of the spirit. After death, the *p'o*
descends into earth while the *hun* ascends into heaven. Cf. 'The
myriad creatures carry on their backs the *yin* and embrace in their
arms the *yang*' (94).

† i.e. the mind.

‡ The gates of heaven are, according to the *Keng sang ch'u*
chapter of the *Chuang tzu*, the invisible gateway through which
the myriad creatures come into being and return to nothing.

XI

27   Thirty spokes
     Share one hub.
  Adapt the nothing therein to the purpose in hand, and
you will have the use of the cart. Knead clay in order
to make a vessel. Adapt the nothing therein to the
purpose in hand, and you will have the use of the
vessel. Cut out doors and windows in order to make
a room. Adapt the nothing* therein to the purpose in
hand, and you will have the use of the room.

27a Thus what we gain is Something, yet it is by virtue of
Nothing that this can be put to use.

---

* In all three cases, by 'nothing' is meant the empty spaces.

XII

28   The five colours make man's eyes blind;
      The five notes make his ears deaf;
      The five tastes injure his palate;
      Riding and hunting
      Make his mind go wild with excitement;
      Goods hard to come by
      Serve to hinder his progress.

29   Hence the sage is
      For the belly
      Not for the eye.

29a Therefore he discards the one and takes the other.

XIII

30 Favour and disgrace are things that startle;
  High rank* is, like one's body, a source of great
   trouble.

30a What is meant by saying that favour and disgrace are
things that startle? Favour when it is bestowed on a
subject serves to startle as much as when it is with-
drawn. This is what is meant by saying that favour
and disgrace are things that startle. What is meant by
saying that high rank is, like one's body, a source of
great trouble? The reason I have great trouble is that
I have a body. When I no longer have a body, what
trouble have I?

31 Hence he who values his body more than dominion
over the empire can be entrusted with the empire.
He who loves his body more than dominion over the
empire can be given the custody of the empire.

* It is probable that the word *kuei* ('high rank') here has
crept in by mistake, since, as it stands, this line has one word more
than the first. If this is the case, then the line should be translated:
'Great trouble is like one's body.' This brings it into line with the
explanation that follows where 'high rank' is not, in fact, mentioned.

XIV

32 What cannot be seen is called evanescent;
  What cannot be heard is called rarefied;
  What cannot be touched is called minute.

32a These three cannot be fathomed
  And so they are confused and looked upon as one.

33 Its upper part is not dazzling;
  Its lower part is not obscure.
  Dimly visible, it cannot be named
  And returns to that which is without substance.
  This is called the shape that has no shape,
  The image that is without substance.
  This is called indistinct and shadowy.
  Go up to it and you will not see its head;
  Follow behind it and you will not see its rear.

34 Hold fast to the way of antiquity
  In order to keep in control the realm of today.
  The ability to know the beginning of antiquity
  Is called the thread running through the way.

XV

35   Of old he who was well versed in the way[1]
Was minutely subtle, mysteriously comprehending,
And too profound to be known.
It is because he could not be known
That he can only be given a makeshift description:
Tentative, as if fording a river in winter,
Hesitant, as if in fear of his neighbours;
Formal like a guest;[2]
Falling apart like thawing ice;
Thick like the uncarved block;
Vacant like a valley;
Murky like muddy water.

36   Who can be muddy and yet, settling, slowly become
        limpid?[3]
Who can be at rest and yet, stirring, slowly come
        to life?
He who holds fast to this way
Desires not to be full.
It is because he is not full
That he can be worn[4] and yet newly made.*

* The present text reads 'That he can be worn and not newly made'. The negative must have crept in by mistake. Cf. 'Worn then new (50).

XVI

37 I do my utmost to attain emptiness;
I hold firmly to stillness.
The myriad creatures all rise together
And I watch their return.
The teaming creatures
All return to their separate roots.
Returning to one's roots is known as stillness.
This is what is meant by returning to one's destiny.
Returning to one's destiny is known as the constant.
Knowledge of the constant is known as discernment.

38 Woe to him who wilfully innovates
While ignorant of the constant,
But should one act from knowledge of the constant
One's action will lead to impartiality,
Impartiality to kingliness,
Kingliness to heaven,
Heaven[1] to the way,
The way to perpetuity,
And to the end of one's days one will meet with no
danger.

XVII

39 The best of all rulers is but a shadowy presence to his
    subjects.
    Next comes the ruler they love and praise;
    Next comes one they fear;
    Next comes one with whom they take liberties.

40 When there is not enough faith, there is lack of good
    faith.

41 Hesitant,[1] he does not utter words lightly.
    When his task is accomplished and his work done
    The people all say, 'It happened to us naturally.'

XVIII

42   When the great way falls into disuse
There are benevolence and rectitude;
When cleverness emerges
There is great hypocrisy;
When the six relations* are at variance
There are filial children;[1]
When the state is benighted
There are loyal ministers.

* The six relations, according to Wang Pi, are father and son, elder and younger brother, husband and wife.

74

XIX

43   Exterminate the sage, discard the wise,
     And the people will benefit a hundredfold;
     Exterminate benevolence, discard rectitude,
     And the people will again be filial;[1]
     Exterminate ingenuity, discard profit,
     And there will be no more thieves and bandits.

43a These three, being false[2] adornments, are not enough
     And the people must have something to which they
         can attach themselves:
     Exhibit the unadorned and embrace the uncarved
         block,
     Have little thought of self and as few desires as
         possible.

XX

44 Exterminate learning and there will no longer be
     worries.*

45 Between yea and nay
    How much difference is there?
    Between good and evil
    How great is the distance?

46 What others fear
    One must also fear.

47 And wax without having reached the limit.†
    The multitude are joyous
    As if partaking of the *t'ai lao*‡ offering
    Or going up to a terrace§ in spring.
    I alone am inactive and reveal no signs,

* This line is clearly out of place in this chapter, and should, almost certainly, form part of the last chapter, but there is disagreement among scholars as to the exact place in the last chapter to which it should be restored. Some believe that it is in fact the last line in that chapter. I am inclined to the view that it should be the first line. In that case, it should also be the first line of 43.

† This line seems unconnected here. Kao Heng suggests that it probably follows on the line 'I alone am inactive and reveal no signs', as both lines are similar not only in their grammatical structure but also in having internal rhymes (*Lao tzu cheng ku*, Peking, 1956, p. 46).

‡ *T'ai lao* is the most elaborate kind of feast, and consists of the three kinds of animals, the ox, the sheep, and the pig.

§ i.e. going on an outing.

Like a baby that has not yet learned to smile,
Listless as though with no home to go back to.
The multitude all have more than enough.
I alone seem to be in want.[1]
My mind is that of a fool – how blank!
Vulgar people are clear.
I alone am drowsy.
Vulgar people are alert.
I alone am muddled.
Calm like the sea;
Like a high wind that never ceases. ||
The multitude all have a purpose.
I alone am foolish and uncouth.
I alone am different from others
And value being fed by the mother.

|| These two lines though seemingly unconnected to the rest of
the section are meant to be a description of the sage, who is
referred to throughout this section in the first person.

XXI

48 In his every movement a man of great virtue
   Follows the way and the way only.

49 As a thing the way is
   Shadowy, indistinct.
   Indistinct and shadowy,
   Yet within it is an image;
   Shadowy and indistinct,
   Yet within it is a substance.
   Dim and dark,
   Yet within it is an essence.
   This essence is quite genuine
   And within it is something that can be tested.

49a From the present back to antiquity[1]
   Its name never deserted it.
   It serves as a means for inspecting the fathers of the
    multitude.

49b How do I know that the fathers of the multitude are
  like that?[2] By means of this.

XXII

50   Bowed down then preserved;
     Bent then straight;
     Hollow then full;
     Worn then new;
     A little then benefited;
     A lot then perplexed.

50a Therefore the sage embraces the One and is a model for the empire.

50b He does not show himself, and so is conspicuous;
     He does not consider himself right, and so is illustrious;
     He does not brag, and so has merit;
     He does not boast, and so endures.

50c It is because he does not contend that no one in the empire is in a position to contend with him.

50d The way the ancients had it, 'Bowed down then preserved', is no empty saying. Truly it enables one to be preserved to the end.

XXIII

51 To use words but rarely
    Is to be natural.

51a Hence a gusty wind cannot last all morning, and a
    sudden downpour cannot last all day. Who is it that
    produces these? Heaven and earth. If even heaven
    and earth cannot go on for ever, much less can man.
    That is why one follows the way.[1]

52 A man of the way conforms to the way; a man of
    virtue conforms to virtue; a man of loss conforms to
    loss. He who conforms to the way is gladly accepted
    by the way; he who conforms to virtue is gladly
    accepted by virtue; he who conforms to loss is gladly
    accepted by loss.*

53 When there is not enough faith, there is lack of good
    faith.

* The word translated 'loss' throughout this section does not make
much sense. It is possible that it is a graphic error for 'heaven', as
suggested by Kao (op. cit., p. 57).

XXIV

54 He who tiptoes cannot stand; he who strides cannot
     walk.

55   He who shows himself is not conspicuous;
         He who considers himself right is not illustrious;
         He who brags will have no merit;
         He who boasts will not endure.

55a From the point of view of the way these are 'excessive
      food and useless excresences'.[1] As there are Things
      that detest them, he who has the way does not abide
      in them.

XXV

56   There is a thing confusedly formed,
     Born before heaven and earth.
     Silent and void
     It stands alone and does not change,
     Goes round and does not weary.
     It is capable of being the mother of the world.
     I know not its name
     So I style it 'the way'.

56a   I give it the makeshift name of 'the great'.
     Being great, it is further described as receding,
     Receding, it is described as far away,
     Being far away, it is described as turning back.

57   Hence the way is great; heaven is great; earth is great; and the king is also great. Within the realm there are four things that are great, and the king counts as one.

58   Man models himself on earth,
     Earth on heaven,
     Heaven on the way,
     And the way on that which is naturally so.

XXVI

59   The heavy is the root of the light;
     The still is the lord of the restless.

59a   Therefore the gentleman[1] when travelling all day
     Never lets the heavily laden carts out of his sight.
     It is only[2] when he is safely behind walls[3] and
       watch-towers
     That he rests peacefully and is above worries.
     How, then, should a ruler of ten thousand chariots
     Make light of his own person in the eyes of the
      empire?

59b   If light, then the root is lost;
     If restless, then the lord is lost.

XXVII

60   One who excels in travelling leaves no wheel tracks;
     One who excels in speech makes no slips;
     One who excels in reckoning uses no counting rods;
     One who excels in shutting uses no bolts yet what he
        has shut cannot be opened;
     One who excels in tying uses no cords yet what he
        has tied cannot be undone.

61   Therefore the sage always excels in saving people, and
     so abandons no one; always excels in saving things,
     and so abandons nothing.

61a This is called following one's discernment.

62   Hence the good man is the teacher the bad learns
        from;
     And the bad man is the material the good works on.
     Not to value the teacher
     Nor to love the material
     Though it seems clever, betrays great bewilderment.

62a This is called the essential and the secret.

XXVIII

63   Know the male
But keep to the role of the female
And be a ravine to the empire.
If you are a ravine to the empire,
Then the constant virtue will not desert you
And you will again return to being a babe.
Know the white
But keep to the role of the black
And be a model to the empire.
If you are a model to the empire,
Then the constant virtue will not be wanting
And you will return to the infinite.
Know honour*
But keep to the role of the disgraced
And be a valley to the empire.
If you are a valley to the empire,
Then the constant virtue will be sufficient
And you will return to being the uncarved block.

* The six lines beginning with 'But keep to the role of the black' are almost certain to be an interpolation, but of an early date. If that is the case, then the line following should be translated 'But keep to the role of the sullied', thus forming a contrast to the line 'Know the white' with which it is continuous. This conjecture is supported by the fact that as quoted in the *T'ien hsia* chapter in the *Chuang tzu* the line 'Know the white' is, in fact, followed by the line 'But keep to the role of the sullied'. Cf. also 'The sheerest whiteness seems sullied' (91).

64 When the uncarved block shatters it becomes vessels.†
The sage makes use of these and becomes the lord
over the officials.

65 Hence the greatest cutting
Does not sever.

---

† i.e. officials whose specialist knowledge and ability make
them fit to be officials but unfit to be rulers. Cf. the phrase 'lord
over the vessels' (164).

XXIX

66 Whoever takes the empire and wishes to do anything
to it I see will have no respite. The empire is a
sacred vessel and nothing should be done to it.
Whoever does anything to it will ruin it; whoever
lays hold of it will lose it.

67 Hence some things lead and some follow;
Some breathe gently and some breathe hard;
Some are strong and some are weak;
Some destroy and some are destroyed.

68 Therefore the sage avoids excess, extravagance, and
arrogance.

XXX

69 One who assists the ruler of men by means of the way does not intimidate the empire by a show of arms.

69a This is something which is liable to rebound.
Where troops have encamped
There will brambles grow;
In the wake of a mighty army
Bad harvests follow without fail.

69b One who[1] is good aims only at bringing his campaign to a conclusion and dare not thereby intimidate. Bring it to a conclusion but do not boast; bring it to a conclusion but do not brag; bring it to a conclusion but do not be arrogant; bring it to a conclusion but only when there is no choice; bring it to a conclusion but do not intimidate.

70 A creature in its prime doing harm*[2] to the old
Is known as going against the way.
That which goes against the way will come to an early end.

* The word in the present text means 'then' and does not make good sense. I have followed the emendation suggested by Kao to a word meaning 'to harm' (op. cit., pp. 71–2).

XXXI*

72   (a) It is because[1] arms are instruments of ill omen and there are Things that detest them that one who has the way does not abide by their use. (b) The gentleman gives precedence to the left when at home, but to the right when he goes to war. Arms are instruments of ill omen, not the instruments of the gentleman. When one is compelled to use them, it is best to do so without relish. There is no glory in victory, and to glorify it despite this is to exult in the killing of men. One who exults in the killing of men will never have his way in the empire. (c) On occasions of rejoicing precedence is given to the left; on occasions of mourning precedence is given to the right. A lieutenant's place is on the left; the general's place is on the right. This means that it is mourning rites that are observed.

* The text of this chapter is obviously in disorder and needs rearrangement, but none of the many suggestions for such rearrangement seems to me to be totally satisfactory. I propose the single transposition of passages which I have marked (a) and (b). There is one further point to be noted. This chapter and chapter LXVI stand out as the two chapters which have no commentary in the existing Wang Pi version. In connexion with this chapter this fact has been variously interpreted. Some think that this means that this chapter is a later interpolation. Others think that Wang's commentary has become mixed up with the text. Still others think that this means at least that Wang suspected the authenticity of the chapter and showed this by leaving it without commentary.

When great numbers of people are killed, one should weep over them with sorrow. When victorious in war, one should observe the rites of mourning.

XXXII

72 The way is for ever nameless.
Though the uncarved block is small
No one in the world dare claim its allegiance.
Should lords and princes be able to hold fast to it
The myriad creatures will submit of their own
accord,
Heaven and earth will unite and sweet dew will fall,
And the people will be equitable, though no one so
decrees.
Only when it is cut are there names.
As soon as there are names
One ought to know that it is time to stop.
Knowing when to stop one can be free from
danger.

73 The way is to the world as the River and the Sea are
to rivulets and streams.

XXXIII

74 He who knows others is clever;
He who knows himself has discernment.
He who overcomes others has force;
He who overcomes himself is strong.

75 He who knows contentment is rich;
He who perseveres is a man of purpose;
He who does not lose his station will endure;
He who lives out his days has had a long life.

XXXIV

76   The way is broad, reaching left as well as right.
     The myriad creatures depend on it for life yet it claims no authority.
     It accomplishes its task yet lays claim to no merit.
     It clothes and feeds the myriad creatures yet lays no claim to being their master.

76a For ever free of desire, it can be called small; yet, as it lays no claim to being master when the myriad creatures turn to it, it can be called great.

76b It is because it never attempts itself to be great that it succeeds in becoming great.

XXXV

77   Have in your hold the great image
And the empire will come to you.
Coming to you and meeting with no harm
It will be safe and sound.
Music and food
Will induce the wayfarer to stop.

78   The way in its passage through the mouth is without
     flavour.
It cannot be seen,
It cannot be heard,
Yet it cannot be exhausted by use.

XXXVI

79   If you would have a thing shrink,
       You must first stretch it;
       If you would have a thing weakened,
       You must first strengthen it;
       If you would have a thing laid aside,
       You must first set it up;
       If you would take from a thing,
       You must first give to it.

79a   This is called subtle discernment:
       The submissive and weak will overcome the hard
         and strong.

80   The fish must not be allowed to leave the deep;
       The instruments of power in a state must not be
         revealed to anyone.*

---

* This section is quoted and commented upon in chapters 21 and 31 of the *Han fei tzu*, but unfortunately the comments are somewhat obscure because the text is probably corrupt. The general point seems to be this. The 'fish' is the symbol for the ruler, and the 'deep' his power. For a ruler to allow the power to slip out of his hands is for the 'fish' to be 'allowed to leave the deep'. Reward and punishment are the 'twin instruments of power in a state', and 'must not be revealed to anyone', lest, in the wrong hands, even the knowledge of how they are dispensed can be turned into a source of power.

XXXVII

81   The way never acts yet nothing is left undone.
      Should lords and princes be able to hold fast to it,
      The myriad creatures will be transformed of their
          own accord.
      After they are transformed, should desire raise its
          head,
      I shall press it down with the weight of the nameless
          uncarved block.
      The nameless uncarved block
      Is but freedom from desire,
      And if I cease to desire and remain still,
      The empire will be at peace of its own accord.

BOOK TWO

82 A man of the highest virtue does not keep to virtue
and that is why he has virtue. A man of the lowest
virtue never strays from virtue and that is why he is
without virtue. The former never acts yet leaves
nothing undone.[1] The latter acts but there are things
left undone.[1] A man of the highest benevolence acts,
but from no ulterior motive. A man of the highest
rectitude acts, but from ulterior motive. A man most
conversant in the rites acts, but when no one responds
rolls up his sleeves and resorts to persuasion by force.

83 Hence when the way was lost there was virtue; when
virtue was lost there was benevolence; when benevolence was lost there was rectitude; when rectitude was
lost there were the rites.

84 The rites are the wearing thin of loyalty and good
    faith
    And the beginning of disorder;
    Foreknowledge is the flowery embellishment of the
    way
    And the beginning of folly.

84a Hence the man of large mind abides in the thick not
in the thin, in the fruit not in the flower.

84b Therefore he discards the one and takes the other.

XXXIX

85   Of old, these came to be in possession of the One:
        Heaven in virtue of the One is limpid;
        Earth in virtue of the One is settled;
        Gods in virtue of the One have their potencies;
        The valley in virtue of the One is full;
        The myriad creatures in virtue of the One are alive;
        Lords and princes in virtue of the One become
            leaders in the empire.
    It is the One[1] that makes these what they are.

85a   Without what makes it limpid heaven might split;
        Without what makes it settled earth might sink;
        Without what gives them their potencies gods might
            spend themselves;
        Without what makes it full the valley might run dry;
        Without what keeps them alive the myriad creatures
            might perish;
        Without what makes them leaders[2] lords and
            princes might fall.

86   Hence the superior must have the inferior as root;
    the high must have the low as base.

86a   Thus lords and princes refer to themselves as
'solitary', 'desolate', and 'hapless'. This is taking the
inferior as root, is it not?

87   Hence the highest renown is without renown,[3]
        Not wishing to be one among many like jade
        Nor to be aloof like stone.

XL

88   Turning back is how the way moves;
     Weakness is the means the way employs.
89   The myriad creatures in the world are born from
     Something, and Something from Nothing.

XLI

90   When the best student hears about the way
He practises it assiduously;
When the average student hears about the way
It seems to him one moment there and gone the next;
When the worst student hears about the way
He laughs out loud.
If he did not laugh
It would be unworthy of being the way.

91   Hence the *Chien yen* has it:
The way that is bright seems dull;
The way that leads forward seems to lead backward;
The way that is even seems rough.
The highest virtue is like the valley;
The sheerest whiteness seems sullied;
Ample virtue seems defective;
Vigorous virtue seems indolent;
Plain virtue[1] seems soiled;
The great square has no corners.
The great vessel takes long to complete;
The great note is rarefied in sound;
The great image has no shape.

92   The way conceals itself in being nameless.
It is the way alone that excels in bestowing and in[2]
accomplishing.

XLII

93 The way begets one; one begets two; two begets three; three begets the myriad creatures.

94 The myriad creatures carry on their backs the *yin* and embrace in their arms the *yang* and are the blending of the generative forces of the two.

95 There are no words which men detest more than 'solitary', 'desolate', and 'hapless', yet lords and princes use these to refer to themselves.

96 Thus a thing is sometimes added to by being diminished and diminished by being added to.

97 What others teach I also teach. 'The violent will not come to a natural end.' I shall take this as my precept.

XLIII

98 The most submissive thing in the world can ride roughshod over the hardest in the world – that which is without substance entering that which has no crevices.

99 That is why I know the benefit of resorting to no action. The teaching that uses no words, the benefit[1] of resorting to no action, these are beyond the understanding of all but a very few in the world.

XLIV

100   Your name or your person,
Which is dearer?
Your person or your goods,
Which is worth more?
Gain or loss,
Which is a greater bane?
That is why excessive meanness
Is sure to lead to great expense;
Too much store
Is sure to end in immense loss.
Know contentment
And you will suffer no disgrace;
Know when to stop
And you will meet with no danger.
You can then endure.

XLV

101   Great perfection seems chipped,
      Yet use will not wear it out;
      Great fullness seems empty,
      Yet use will not drain it;
      Great straightness seems bent;
      Great skill seems awkward;
      Great eloquence seems tongue-tied.

102   Restlessness overcomes cold; stillness overcomes heat.

103   Limpid and still,
      One can be a leader in the empire.

XLVI

104   When the way prevails in the empire, fleet-footed horses are relegated to ploughing the fields; when the way does not prevail in the empire, war-horses breed on the border.

105   There is no crime greater than having too many desires;[1]

There is no disaster greater than not being content;

There is no misfortune greater than being covetous.

105a   Hence in being content,[2] one will always have enough.

XLVII

106   Without stirring abroad
One can know the whole world;
Without looking out of the window
One can see the way of heaven.
The further one goes
The less one knows.[1]

107   Therefore the sage knows without having to stir,[2]
Identifies without having to see,
Accomplishes without having to act.

XLVIII

108 In the pursuit of learning one knows more every day;
in the pursuit of the way one does less every day.
One does less and less until one does nothing at all,
and when one does nothing at all there is nothing that
is undone.

109 It is always through not meddling that the empire is
won. Should you meddle, then you are not equal to
the task of winning the empire.

XLIX

110   The sage has no mind of his own. He takes as his own the mind of the people.

111   Those who are good I treat as good. Those who are not good I also treat as good. In so doing I gain in goodness. Those who are of good faith I have faith in. Those who are lacking in good faith I also have faith in. In so doing I gain in good faith.

112   The sage in his attempt to distract the mind of the empire seeks urgently to muddle it. The people all have something to occupy their eyes and ears,[1] and the sage treats them all like children.

L

113 When going one way means life and going the other means death, three in ten will be comrades of life, three in ten will be comrades of death, and there are those who value life[1] and as a result move into the realm of death, and these also number three in ten.* Why is this so? Because they set too much store by life. I have heard it said that one who excels in safeguarding his own life does not meet with rhinoceros or tiger when travelling on land nor is he touched by weapons when charging into an army. There is nowhere for the rhinoceros to pitch its horn; there is nowhere for the tiger to place its claws; there is nowhere for the weapon to lodge its blade. Why is this so? Because for him there is no realm of death.

---

* 'Three in ten' is a rough way of saying 'one third'.

LI

114   The way gives them life;
        Virtue rears them;
        Things give them shape;
        Circumstances bring them to maturity.

114a   Therefore the myriad creatures all revere the way and
        honour virtue. Yet the way is revered and virtue
        honoured not because this is decreed by any authority
        but because it is natural for them to be treated so.

115   Thus the way gives them life and rears[1] them;
        Brings them up and nurses them;
        Brings them to fruition and maturity;
        Feeds and shelters them.

116   It gives them life yet claims no possession;
        It benefits them yet exacts no gratitude;
        It is the steward yet exercises no authority.
        Such is called the mysterious virtue.

LII

117 The world had a beginning
And this beginning could[1] be the mother of the
world.
When you know the mother
Go on to know the child.
After you have known the child
Go back to holding fast to the mother,
And to the end of your days you will not meet with
danger.

118 Block the openings,
Shut the doors,*
And all your life you will not run dry.
Unblock the openings,
Add to your troubles,
And to the end of your days you will be beyond
salvation.

119 To see the small is called discernment;
To hold fast to the submissive is called strength.
Use the light
But give up the discernment.
Bring not misfortune upon yourself.

119a This is known as following the constant.[2]

* 'Openings' and 'doors' refer to the senses and the intelligence.

LIII

120   Were I possessed of the least knowledge, I would, when walking on the great way, fear only paths that lead astray. The great way is easy, yet people prefer by-paths.

121   The court is corrupt,
     The fields are overgrown with weeds,
     The granaries are empty;
     Yet there are those dressed in fineries,
     With swords at their sides,
     Filled with food and drink,
     And possessed of too much wealth.
     This is known as taking the lead in robbery.

121a   Far indeed is this from the way.

LIV

122   What is firmly rooted cannot be pulled out;
What is tightly held in the arms will not slip loose;
Through this the offering of sacrifice by descendants
    will never come to an end.

123   Cultivate it in your person
And its virtue will be genuine;
Cultivate it in the family
And its virtue will be more than sufficient;
Cultivate it in the hamlet
And its virtue will endure;
Cultivate it in the state
And its virtue will abound;
Cultivate it in the empire
And its virtue will be pervasive.

124   Hence look at the person through the person; look
at the family through the family; look at the hamlet
through the hamlet; look at the state through the
state; look at the empire through the empire.

124a How do I know that the empire is like that? By means
of this.

LV

125　One who possesses virtue in abundance is comparable to a new born babe:

　　Poisonous insects[1] will not sting it;

　　Ferocious animals will not pounce on it;

　　Predatory birds will not swoop down on it.

　　Its bones are weak and its sinews supple yet its hold is firm.

　　It does not know of the union of[2] male and female yet its male member[3] will stir:

　This is because its virility is at its height.

　　It howls all day yet does not become hoarse:

　This is because its harmony is at its height.

126　To know harmony is called the constant;

　　To know the constant is called discernment.

　　To try to add to one's vitality is called ill-omened;

　　For the mind to egg on the breath is called violent.

127　A creature in its prime doing harm to the old

　　Is known as going against the way.

　　That which goes against the way will come to an early end.*

* This section is identical with section 70 and the text has been emended in the same way.

LVI

128   One who knows does not speak; one who speaks
does not know.

129   Block the openings;
    Shut the doors.
    Blunt the sharpness;
    Untangle the knots;
    Soften the glare;
    Let your wheels move only along old ruts.

129a   This is known as mysterious sameness.

130   Hence you cannot get close to it, nor can you keep
it at arm's length; you cannot bestow benefit on it,
nor can you do it harm; you cannot ennoble it, nor
can you debase it.

130a   Therefore it is valued by the empire.

LVII

131   Govern the state by being straightforward; wage war by being crafty; but win the empire by not being meddlesome.

131a How do I know that it is like that? By means of this.

132   The more taboos there are in the empire
      The poorer the people;
      The more sharpened tools the people have
      The more benighted the state;
      The more skills the people have
      The further novelties multiply;
      The better known the laws and edicts
      The more thieves and robbers there are.

133   Hence the sage says,
      I take no action and the people are transformed of
          themselves;
      I prefer stillness and the people are rectified of
          themselves;
      I am not meddlesome and the people prosper of
          themselves;
      I am free from desire and the people of themselves
          become simple like the uncarved block.

LVIII

134 When the government is muddled
The people are simple;
When the government is alert
The people are cunning.

135 It is on disaster that good fortune perches;
It is beneath good fortune that disaster crouches.

135a Who knows the limit? Does not the straightforward
exist? The straightforward changes again into the
crafty, and the good changes again into the monstrous.
Indeed, it is long since the people were perplexed.

136 Therefore the sage is square-edged but does not
scrape,
Has corners but does not jab,
Extends himself but not at the expense of others,
Shines but does not dazzle.

LIX

137   In ruling the people and in serving heaven it is best
      for a ruler to be sparing.

It is because he is sparing

That he may be said to follow the way from the
      start;

Following the way from the start he may be said to
      accumulate an abundance of virtue;

Accumulating an abundance of virtue there is
      nothing he cannot overcome;

When there is nothing he cannot overcome, no one
      knows his limit;

When no one knows his limit

He can possess a state;[1]

When he possesses the mother of a state

He can then endure.

This is called the way of deep roots and firm stems
      by which one lives to see many days.

LX

138   Governing a large state is like boiling a small fish.*

139   When the empire is ruled in accordance with the way,
     The spirits lose their potencies.
     Or rather, it is not that they lose their potencies,
     But that, though they have their potencies, they do
       not harm the people.
     It is not only they who, having their potencies, do
       not harm the people,
     The sage, also, does not harm the people.
     As neither does any harm, each attributes the merit
     to the other.

* This is because a small fish can be spoiled simply by being handled.

LXI

140   A large state is the lower reaches of a river –
       The place where all the streams of the world unite.*

141   In the union[1] of the world,
       The female always gets the better of the male by
          stillness.

141a   Being still, she takes the lower position.

142   Hence the large state, by taking the lower position,
          annexes the small state;
       The small state, by taking the lower position,
          affiliates itself to the large state.

142a   Thus the one, by taking the lower position, annexes;
       The other, by taking the lower position, is annexed.
       All that the large state wants is to take the other
          under its wing;
       All that the small state wants is to have its services
          accepted by the other.
       If each of the two wants to find its proper place,[2]
       It is meet that the large should take the lower
          position.

* cf. section 159.

LXIV

152   It is easy to maintain a situation while it is still
      secure;
    It is easy to deal with a situation before symptoms
      develop;
    It is easy to break a thing when it is yet brittle;
    It is easy to dissolve a thing when it is yet minute.

152a Deal with a thing while it is still nothing;
    Keep a thing in order before disorder sets in.

153   A tree that can fill the span of a man's arms
    Grows from a downy tip;[1]
    A terrace nine storeys high
    Rises from hodfuls of earth;
    A journey of a thousand miles
    Starts from beneath one's feet.

154   Whoever does anything to it will ruin it; whoever
    lays hold of it will lose it.

154a Therefore the sage, because he does nothing, never
    ruins anything; and, because he does not lay hold of
    anything, loses nothing.

155   In their enterprises the people
    Always ruin them when on the verge of success.
    Be as careful at the end as at the beginning
    And there will be no ruined enterprises.

156   Therefore the sage desires not to desire
    And does not value goods which are hard to come
      by;

Learns to be without learning
And makes good the mistakes of the multitude
In order to help the myriad creatures to be natural
   and to refrain from daring to act.

LXV

157   Of old those who excelled in the pursuit of the way
did not use it to enlighten the people but to hoodwink
them. The reason why the people are difficult to
govern is that they are too clever.

158   Hence to rule a state by cleverness
Will be to the detriment of the state;
Not to rule a state by cleverness
Will be a boon to the state.
These two are models.[1]
Always to know the models
Is known as mysterious virtue.
Mysterious virtue is profound and far-reaching,
But when things turn back it turns back with them.

158a   Only then is complete conformity realized.

LXVI

159　The reason why the River and the Sea are able to be king of the hundred valleys is that they excel in taking the lower position. Hence they are able to be king of the hundred valleys.

160　Therefore, desiring to rule over the people,
　　One must in one's words humble oneself before them;
　　And, desiring to lead the people,
　　One must, in one's person, follow behind them.

161　Therefore the sage takes his place over the people yet is no burden; takes his place ahead of the people yet causes no obstruction. That is why the empire supports him joyfully and never tires of doing so.

162　It is because he does not contend that no one in the empire is in a position to contend with him.

LXVII

163 The whole world says that my way is vast and resembles nothing. It is because it is vast that it resembles nothing. If it resembled anything, it would, long before now, have become small.

164 I have three treasures
Which I hold and cherish.
The first is known as compassion,
The second is known as frugality,
The third is known as not daring to take the lead in the empire;
Being compassionate one could afford to be courageous,
Being frugal one could afford to extend one's territory,
Not daring to take the lead in the empire one could afford to be lord over the vessels.*

164a Now, to forsake compassion for courage, to forsake frugality for expansion, to forsake the rear for the lead, is sure to end in death.

165 Through compassion, one will triumph in attack and be impregnable in defence. What heaven succours it protects with the gift of compassion.

* i.e. officials. Cf. section 64 and the note to it.

LXVIII

166   One who excels as a warrior does not appear
            formidable;
        One who excels in fighting is never roused in anger;
        One who excels in defeating his enemy does not
            join issue;
        One who excels in employing others humbles him-
            self before them.

166a   This is known as the virtue of non-contention;
        This is known as making use of the efforts of others;
        This is known as matching the sublimity of heaven.[1]

LXIX

167   The strategists have a saying,
        I dare not play the host but play the guest,*
        I dare not advance an inch but retreat a foot instead.

168   This is known as marching forward when there is
           no road,
        Rolling up one's sleeves when there is no arm,
        Dragging one's adversary by force when there is
           no adversary,
        And taking up arms when there are no arms.[1]

169   There is no disaster greater than taking on an enemy
    too easily. So doing nearly cost me my treasure. Thus
    of two sides raising arms against each other, it is the
    one that is sorrow-stricken that wins.

* As against the 'guest', the 'host' is the side that is on its home
ground and with which the initiative rests.

LXX

170   My words are very easy to understand and very easy to put into practice, yet no one in the world can understand them or put them into practice.

171   Words have an ancestor and affairs have a sovereign.*

172   It is because people are ignorant that they fail to understand me.

     Those who understand me are few;

     Those who imitate† me are honoured.

172a Therefore the sage, while clad in homespun, conceals on his person a priceless piece of jade.

---

* If one could only grasp the 'ancestor' and the 'sovereign', then the understanding of all words and all affairs will follow.

† The word here translated as 'imitate' is the same as the word translated as 'then' in section 70. It is likely that, as in that section, this is also a corruption from the word meaning 'harm' (see Kao, op. cit., p. 140). If that is the case, it is much easier to see the relevance of what is said about the sage in the next section.

LXXI

173   To know yet to think that one does not know is best;
Not to know yet to think that one knows will lead
to difficulty.

173a It is by being alive to difficulty that one can avoid it.
The sage meets with no difficulty. It is because he is
alive to it that he meets with no difficulty.

LXXII

174 When the people lack a proper sense of awe, then some awful visitation will descend upon them.

175 Do not constrict their living space; do not press down on their means of livelihood. It is because you do not press down on them that they will not weary of the burden.

176 Hence the sage knows himself but does not display himself, loves himself but does not exalt himself.

176a Therefore he discards the one and takes the other.

LXXIII

177　He who is fearless in being bold will meet with his
　　　　death;
　　　He who is fearless in being timid will stay alive.
　　　Of the two, one leads to good, the other to harm.
178　Heaven hates what it hates,
　　　Who knows the reason why?
178a　Therefore even the sage treats some things as
　　　difficult.
179　The way of heaven
　　　Excels in overcoming though it does not contend,
　　　In responding though it does not speak,
　　　In attracting though it does not summon,
　　　In laying plans though it appears slack.
179a　The net of heaven is cast wide. Though the mesh is
　　　not fine, yet nothing ever slips through.

LXXIV

180   When the people are not afraid of death, wherefore frighten them with death? Were the people always afraid of death, and were I able to arrest and put to death those who innovate, then who would dare? There is a regular executioner whose charge it is to kill. To kill on behalf of the executioner is what is described as chopping wood on behalf of the master carpenter. In chopping wood on behalf of the master carpenter, there are few who escape hurting their own hands instead.

LXXV

181   The people are hungry:
      It is because those in authority eat up too much in taxes
      That the people are hungry.
      The people are difficult to govern:
      It is because those in authority are too fond of action
      That the people are difficult to govern.
      The people treat death lightly:
      It is because the people set too much store by life[1]
      That they treat death lightly.

181a It is just because one has no use for life that one is wiser than the man who values life.

LXXVI

182   A man is supple and weak when living, but hard and stiff when dead. Grass and trees[1] are pliant and fragile when living, but dried and shrivelled when dead. Thus the hard and the strong are the comrades of death; the supple and the weak are the comrades of life.

183   Therefore a weapon that is strong will not vanquish;
A tree that is strong will suffer the axe.[2]
The strong and big takes the lower position,
The supple and weak takes the higher position.*

* Throughout this chapter the words used in the Chinese are *jou* and *ch'iang*, but in the translation the former is translated as 'supple' and as 'pliant', while the latter is translated as 'stiff' and as 'strong'. Elsewhere in the book, *jou* is also translated as 'submissive'.

LXXVII

184 Is not the way of heaven like the stretching* of a bow?
    The high it presses down,
    The low it lifts up;
    The excessive it takes from,
    The deficient it gives to.

184a It is the way of heaven to take from what has in excess in order to make good what is deficient. The way of man is otherwise. It takes from those who are in want in order to offer this to those who already have more than enough. Who is there that can take what he himself has in excess and offer this to the empire? Only he who has the way.

185   Therefore the sage benefits them yet exacts no
        gratitude,
    Accomplishes his task yet lays claim to no merit.

185a Is this not because he does not wish to be considered a better man than others?

* In order to test the bow and to correct any faults that may appear.

LXXVIII

186 In the world there is nothing more submissive and weak than water. Yet for attacking that which is hard and strong nothing can surpass it. This is because[1] there is nothing that can take its place.

187 That the weak overcomes the strong,
And the submissive overcomes the hard,
Everyone in the world knows yet no one can put this knowledge into practice.

188 Therefore the sage says,
One who takes on himself the humiliation of the state
Is called a ruler worthy of offering sacrifices to the gods of earth and millet;*
One who takes on himself the calamity of the state
Is called a king worthy of dominion over the entire empire.

189 Straightforward words
Seem paradoxical.

* Each state has its own shrines to the gods of earth and millet, and a state remains independent only so long as its ruler is able to maintain these shrines.

LXXIX

190   When peace is made between great enemies,
      Some enmity is bound to remain undispelled.
      How can this be considered perfect?

191   Therefore the sage takes the left-hand tally,* but
      exacts no payment from the people.
      The man of virtue takes charge of the tally;
      The man of no virtue takes charge of exaction.†

192   It is the way of heaven to show no favouritism.
      It is for ever on the side of the good man.

---

* The left-hand tally is the half held by the creditor.
† The reading *ch'e* 'exaction' here is difficult. It is possible that Kao is right in suggesting that it should be emended to *sha*, 'to kill' (op. cit., p. 150). If that is the case the translation will become 'takes charge of execution'.

LXXX

193   Reduce the size and population of the state. Ensure that even though the people have tools of war for a troop or a battalion they will not use them; and also that they will be reluctant to move to distant places because they look on death as no light matter.

193a   Even when they have ships and carts, they will have no use for them; and even when they have armour and weapons, they will have no occasion to make a show of them.

193b   Bring it about that the people will return to the use of the knotted rope,
    Will find relish in their food
    And beauty in their clothes,
    Will be content in their abode
    And happy in the way they live.

193c   Though adjoining states are within sight of one another, and the sound of dogs barking and cocks crowing in one state can be heard in another, yet the people of one state will grow old and die without having had any dealings with those of another.

LXXXI

194 Truthful words are not beautiful; beautiful words are not truthful. Good words are not persuasive; persuasive words are not good. He who knows has no wide learning; he who has wide learning does not know.

195 The sage does not hoard.

Having bestowed all he has on others, he has yet more;

Having given all he has to others, he is richer still.

196 The way of heaven benefits and does not harm; the way of the sage is bountiful and does not contend.

LIST OF PASSAGES FOR

COMPARISON (see p. 168)

3a, 129a

6, 99; 10, 81, 82, 108, 147

7, 26, 76, 116, 185

8, 28, 156

9, 112, 157

11, 17, 78, 101

12, 118, 129

19, 160

22, 50c, 162

24, 63

26, 158

29a, 84b, 176a

30a, 181a

32, 91 (end)

33, 49

36 (end), 50, 101

37, 119, 126

38 (end), 117 (end)

40, 53, 111; 61, 145

41, 51

49b, 124a, 131a

50b, 55

55a, 71

56a, 88, 158

59, 59b, 102

61a, 62a, 79a, 119a

63, 91

64, 164, 72 (end)

66, 154

70, 127

71 (end), 169

72, 81; 76a, 133

72 (end), 100 (end), 105, 105a

76b, 150

78, 147

79a, 98, 186, 187

86a, 95

109, 131, 133

113, 181 (end)

121, 181

128, 194

130a, 146a

140, 159

141ff., 183

151a, 178a; 173a

161, 175

170, 187

182 (end), 113

THE PROBLEM OF AUTHORSHIP

The most difficult problem in dealing with the history of Chinese thought in the ancient period is how to establish the approximate dates of the various philosophers and philosophical works so that a rough chronological order may be decided on, which is essential to an understanding of the historical development. For instance, given two philosophical works, A and B, the way the thought contained in them is interpreted if A is earlier than B often has to be radically changed if it is shown that B is, in fact, earlier than A. The interpretation of the *Lao tzu* is a case in point. This depends on whether we accept the traditional view that it was written by Lao Tzu who was an older contemporary of Confucius and so was a work of the sixth century B.C., or the view favoured by a great number of modern scholars which would place the work in the late fourth or early third century B.C. For this reason it is vital to our task of correctly interpreting the thought in the *Lao tzu* to examine the soundness of the traditional view.*

The traditional view is based on the fact that a meeting was supposed to have taken place between Confucius and Lao Tzu, and the earliest historical work that contains an account of such a meeting is the *Shih chi*. In both the biography of Lao Tzu and that of Confucius in this work, the account begins with Confucius going to Chou to put questions to Lao Tzu concerning the rites, but in the actual account nothing further is said about

---

* To help the reader to follow the argument a chronological table is provided on p. 175.

the rites. All that takes place is a lecture from Lao Tzu on the kind of behaviour to be avoided. This seems to show that Ssu-ma Chi'en must have used two distinct sources, one concerning Confucius receiving instruction in the rites which, as we shall see, is of Confucianist origin, and the other concerning the censure of Confucius by Lao Tzu which is of Taoist origin. Although we no longer have the sources that Ssu-ma Ch'ien used, fortunately we have accounts concerning the meeting in two extant works. On the one hand, we have in the *Chuang tzu* accounts of the meeting and of the censure of Confucius by Lao Tzu. On the other, in the *Li chi* (*Records of Rites*), a Confucianist work compiled in the first century B.C., we have four instances of Confucius recalling what he learned about the rites from Lao Tzu, though there is no account of the actual meeting.

In the *Chuang tzu* there are several versions of the story, and though these all differ considerably from those in the *Shih chi*, they are, as is the case with the *Shih chi* accounts, of Taoist origin. The *Li chi* passages concern the rites only, but, as the *Shih chi* does no more than mention the rites, they serve to give us some idea of the nature of the points of rites involved and the kind of sources the *Shih chi* might have used. Because both the *Shih chi* and the *Li chi* are of comparatively late date, and the *Li chi* does not contain an account of the actual meeting between the two, far more weight has been attached to the *Chuang tzu*, and it is upon the accounts in the *Chuang tzu* that the traditionalists' case rests. It is argued that as accounts of the encounter between Lao Tzu and Confucius are to be found in the *Chuang tzu*, the story, at least, of such an encounter must have existed at the time of Chuang Tzu, and the man Lao Tzu must have existed before Chuang Tzu, and the book *Lao tzu* must have been written, even if the story is untrue, before the end of the fourth century B.C., but as early as the sixth century if the story is true. Needless to say, this argument is highly unsatisfactory, as it rests on the simple but questionable assumption that the *Chuang tzu* was written by Chuang Tzu and the *Lao tzu* by Lao Tzu, with no more grounds than that these books are traditionally thought to have been named after their authors. It is further argued that as accounts are found in the *Chuang tzu* it follows that Chuang Tzu knew of Lao Tzu, and from this it is concluded that the book *Lao tzu* must have existed in the time of Chuang Tzu. Moreover, it is assumed that if the story was current in Chuang Tzu's time, even if this was no more than a story, it established the priority in time of Lao Tzu over Chuang Tzu. This is to ignore the possibility that Lao Tzu might not have been a historical personage at all.

Let us take the assumption that the *Lao tzu* was written by Lao Tzu and the *Chuang tzu* by Chuang Tzu. This is an exceedingly questionable assumption and has to be carefully examined. In order to do this, we must make a digression and say something about the way books were compiled in ancient China.

The earliest works, as is well known, are collections of the sayings of particular thinkers which must have undergone more than once the process of compilation in the hands of disciples and their disciples in turn, and so on. These works came, at some time or other, to be known by the name of the thinkers in question. Practically all ancient philosophical works are so named, with the exception of the collection of sayings by Confucius which was known as the *Lun yü*.

Within the same work, another principle of compilation seemed to have operated as well. Passages that have something in common, a common topic or a common interlocutor, for instance, are placed together. It is not clear at what date this principle came to be adopted, but we can find examples of this in the *Analects of Confucius* and in the *Mencius*. For instance, in Book 4 of the *Analects*, sections 1 to 6 all deal with 'benevolence', and sections 18 to 21 with 'filial conduct', while in the *Mencius* Book 5 Part I consists solely of answers given by Mencius to questions expressing doubt over accepted traditions concerning sage kings. This principle was not only followed but explicitly stated by Liu Hsiang at the end of the first century B.C. when he edited the *Shuo yüan* and the *Hsin hsü*. Each of these two works are divided into a number of books, and each book comprises passages concerning a common topic. (Indeed this principle survived in the compilation of encyclopedias ('*lei shu*') in later times.) One suspects that parts of the *Chuang tzu*, for instance, were compiled on this principle as well, though this fact has been obscured by subsequent re-editing. We can still see that the chapter *Jang wang* (Abdication) consists of a number of stories concerning the abdication of the various legendary sage kings, though some extraneous matter has been introduced, while at the same time some of the abdication stories have found their way to other chapters.

In the case of stories, there are some instances where editors have not only placed those that are of the same kind together but have even included variant versions of the same story. These may be slightly different stories about the same characters or similar stories about different characters. This practice can be most clearly seen in, for instance, the *Han fei tzu*, particularly in chapters 30 to 35, where variant versions are often introduced by the formula 'one version has it'.

It is obvious, if books were compiled on such a principle, that material from alien sources and possibly of a considerably later date might easily find its way into a work in spite of the fact that the work is named after a particular thinker and indeed represents in the main the thought of that thinker or at least his school. There are reasons for thinking that this happened more often with works of the later part of the Warring States period, say, from the beginning of the third century B.C., than with works of the preceding period. Earlier works, viz. the *Analects of Confucius* and the *Mencius*, not only consist of sayings by a particular philosopher, but these are invariably introduced by the formula 'Master So-and-so said' or simply 'The Master said' in the case of the *Analects*, and although passages with a common topic are placed together they remain distinctly separate sayings. Furthermore, the formula, though it can obviously never guarantee the authenticity of a saying, nevertheless serves as a sign that the saying was at one time accepted as a saying of the Master, thus rendering it difficult, if not impossible, for alien material to have been incorporated *by accident*.

Again, most of the passages consist of serious discussions about moral and political problems. The occasional story is used only to illustrate a point under discussion. The impression one gets in reading these works is that the sayings were taken down by disciples to whom the memory of the Master was sacred. The result is that these sayings truly reflect both the thought and the style of the man. We feel we are listening to the individual voice of a thinker whose thought exhibits a high degree of unity. There is bound to be material which was probably of a later date, but even this is still material belonging to the same school, though it may belong to a tradition somewhat further removed from the Master. In the case of Mencius, we are probably fortunate in having only a version of his works with all books of a doubtful nature removed by the editor of the third century A.D. Confucius is a more complicated case, because at a very early stage he became known as a sage and so attracted the attribution of apocryphal sayings and the invention of apocryphal stories. But even the inclusion of these, because they are invented deliberately, is quite different from the inclusion of totally alien material by accident.

All this was changed in the case of later works like the *Chuang tzu* and the *Hsün tzu*. These works no longer consist of a series of short sayings introduced by the formula 'Master So-and-so said'. In fact the name of the thinker after whom the work is known figures but rarely. In the *Chuang tzu*, Chuang Tzu's name appears far less frequently than those of the legendary kings Yao and Shun and even that of Confucius. In the *Hsün tzu*, which is a work of considerable length, Hsün Tzu's name occurs in no more than half a dozen or so passages where actual conversations in which Hsün Tzu took part are recorded. Moreover, short sayings have given way to much longer passages, which are often couched in the deceptive form of a continuous exposition. It is only when one examines these passages carefully that one realizes that they are very often actually compiled out of shorter units which are only loosely connected and sometimes not connected at all. This lack of connexion is often disguised by the appearance of connecting words like *ku* (therefore) and *shih yi* (hence). This is a point to which we shall return.

In this respect, the first thirty-five chapters of the *Mo tzu* stand half way between the *Analects* and the *Mencius* on the one hand, and the later works on the other. These chapters in the *Mo tzu* seem to contain continuous exposition, though, in fact, they consist of independent units which have been put together. These shorter units are often of such generality that they can be used equally in a number of contexts. But in one respect the *Mo tzu* is still akin to the *Analects* and the *Mencius*. The formula 'Master So-and-so said' is still to be found, at least at the beginning of each chapter. This, together with the distinctive style of Mohist writing, is to a certain extent a reassurance that the material, though it underwent subsequent editing, is more or less homogeneous and belongs to the same school. In the case of the later works we no longer have such reassurance, particularly where the text is corrupt. The *Chuang tzu*, with which we are immediately concerned, is a case in point. The state of the text is exceedingly corrupt, and it would be over-sanguine not to expect a good deal of alien material to have found its way into such a work. In some chapters there are parts, for instance the end of chapters 23 to 26, which give the impression that not only extraneous matter has been incorporated but that the text has been compiled from broken bamboo slips* so fragmentary in nature as to make no sense whatsoever as they stand.

---

* Bamboo was the common writing material in ancient China. It was cut into narrow slips on which columns of characters were written. These slips were then strung together by cords to form a book which was in effect like a curtain that has been turned sideways. It often happens that the cords rotted with time and that some of the slips got broken at the ends as well. In that case, an editor might have to put together, to the best of his ability, a bundle of loose and at times broken slips. It is not surprising that some of these broken slips found their way into the wrong books.

There is one other feature of these later works. In some of them, there is an increasing tendency to use stories for the sake of the moral in them. These stories are no longer used in the context of an actual argument as in the earlier works, but are entirely independent. In such cases, it is difficult to find any marks of authorship or of origin, particularly when slightly different versions of the same story sometimes occur in more than one work.

It is possible that if a detailed study were made of such stories they could be grouped into categories according to their form. But a discussion of this problem will take us too far afield. The category that has special relevance for our immediate purpose is what may be called the illustrative story. An illustrative story is a story which is told for its point, and this is the only factor which matters and which remains constant while other factors may vary from version to version. These include the identity of the characters other than the main character, the location of the story and so on. We shall return to this point.

To go back to the works of the latter part of the Warring States period. Because of the features that we have seen, unless there are strong reasons, it is never safe to assume that any such work was actually written by a particular thinker or even that the whole work represents a single tradition in a closely knit school. It is far safer to assume that it is an anthology which passed through the hands of a compiler or of a series of compilers, in the course of time. The judgement of the compilers need not always be sound, and the fact that passages are placed together need not have very much to do with their contents. Although in the majority of cases such passages deal with a common topic, it sometimes happens that these have nothing more in common than one or more catchwords and the point made in each passage is quite different.

I hope enough has been said to show that it is not safe to assume that the *Chuang tzu* was written by Chuang Tzu simply because such an attribution is traditional. If that is so, we cannot assume, because Lao Tzu is mentioned in the *Chuang tzu*, that Chuang Tzu must have known of him. In fact what we are entitled to is simply the tautological statement that the parts of the *Chuang tzu* which contain stories about Lao Tzu must have been written at a time when the stories were already current. All we have done is to exchange the problem about the date of Lao Tzu for the problem about the date of the parts of the *Chuang tzu* which contain stories about Lao Tzu, and even then, what we can hope to settle, assuming for argument's sake that we can come to any definite conclusions about the date of these parts of the *Chuang tzu*, is the date of the currency of the stories, not the date of Lao Tzu the man.

Although the mere fact that stories concerning Lao Tzu are to be found in the *Chuang tzu* does not entitle us to answer the question, 'did Chuang Tzu know of Lao Tzu?' it is nevertheless an interesting question and one that we ought to ask. One of the strongest arguments against the traditionalists' case for placing Lao Tzu in the sixth century B.C. is the fact that Mencius, in spite of his strong sense of mission against heterodox schools, attacks Yang Chu and Mo Tzu but does not mention Lao Tzu. Not only does he not mention Lao Tzu explicitly, but he never even shows any awareness of any of the views we associate with Lao Tzu. The traditionalists' answer often takes the form that, although Mencius did not mention Lao Tzu, Chuang Tzu certainly did. We have seen that the force of the argument depends on whether by 'Chuang Tzu' is meant the work or the man. If the work is meant the fact is undeniable but proves nothing. But if the man is meant, then the question is an interesting one and should be examined.

In order to answer this question, we have to re-formulate it and ask: in passages in the *Chuang tʒu* where Chuang Tzu figures in a serious philosophical discussion does he ever mention, or, in general, show any signs that he knows of Lao Tzu? The answer to this is no. It may be said that in the passages where Chuang Tzu figures, perhaps there is no reason for him to mention Lao Tzu. This may be true of some of these passages, but there is one passage where Chuang Tzu's silence on the point is, to say the least, surprising. In chapter 24 there is a conversation between Chuang Tzu and his friend, the famous sophist, Hui Shih. Chuang Tzu said, 'Ju, Mo, Yang, and Ping are four. Together with you it will make five.' Leaving on one side the question as to who Ping was – and the answer is certainly not relevant to our question – Chuang Tzu has named only three schools of thought, viz. Ju, i.e. the Confucian school, Mo, i.e. the school of Mo Tzu, and Yang, i.e. the school of Yang Chu. Why did Chuang Tzu not mention Lao Tzu and his school, particularly as, according to the traditionalist view, Chuang Tzu was the second great Taoist thinker who carried on the teachings of the school founded by Lao Tzu? This silence seems to go some way in providing evidence to show that Chuang Tzu was not aware either of Lao Tzu or of his school or, at least, not as a prominent school of thought dating from the time of Confucius.

Although we can proceed no further with the problem as far as the *Chuang tʒu* is concerned, there is one piece of evidence which is relevant. In chapter 3 of the *Mo tzu*, Mo Tzu was said to have been moved by the sight of silk coming out the colour of the dye. This was taken as a moral the application of which could be extended to the state and the individual. When the king of a state is influenced by good ministers, that state will be well governed. When an individual is influenced by good teachers and friends, he will be a good man. Examples are given in each case. Now this chapter is to be found also in the *Lü shih ch'un ch'iu* (chüan 3, pt 4), and the two versions are in fact identical up to the end of the section about the 'dyeing' of states. The final section about individuals is quite different. In the *Mo tzu* version three examples only are given of individuals who came under the influence of good men, viz. Tuan-kan Mu, Ch'in Ku-li and Fu Yüeh. Tuan-kan Mu was a Confucian and Ch'in Ku-li a well-known disciple of Mo Tzu's, both of the fifth century B.C. (Fu Yüeh was an ancient figure and does not concern us). In the *Lü shih ch'un ch'iu*, however, the list is augmented, and at the head of this list of illustrious individuals is Confucius who was said to have come under the good influence of, amongst others, Lao Tzu. It seems that between the time the *Mo tzu* chapter assumed its present form and the time it was incorporated, in its modified form, into the *Lü shih ch'un ch'iu*, the story of Confucius receiving instruction from Lao Tzu must have become so well known that in revising the list the editors of the *Lü shih ch'un ch'iu* placed Confucius at the head of it. As we know roughly the date of composition of the *Lü shih ch'un ch'iu*, if we could determine approximately the *terminus a quo* of the *Mo tzu* chapter we can determine the period in which the story gained currency. This we are fortunately in a position to do. The *Mo tzu* chapter mentions the death of King K'ang of Sung which took place in 286 B.C. Thus we can say that the chapter could not have been completed in its present form before that date, although there is no reason to doubt the authenticity of the saying attributed to Mo Tzu in the opening section. We can say, then, that it must have been within the period of the forty years or so between 286 and 240 B.C. that the story of the encounter between Confucius and Lao Tzu became widely known and accepted.

We can sum up our somewhat lengthy discussion so far of the problem of whether Lao Tzu was a historical figure who lived in the sixth century B.C., in this way. Not only did Mencius show no signs of awareness of Lao Tzu and his school, Chuang Tzu who lived probably well on into the third century B.C. showed no knowledge of Lao Tzu either. This is surprising in the case of Mencius for he was such a staunch supporter of the Confucian philosophy and was tireless in his attacks on heterodox views, and it is equally surprising in the case of Chuang Tzu for, according to the traditionalist account, he was the successor to Lao Tzu in the Taoist school of thought. We have seen that it was not until the second half of the third century B.C. that the story of an encounter between Lao Tzu and Confucius became widely known. And it is solely on this story that the traditionalists' case for Lao Tzu being an older contemporary of Confucius is founded.

Apart from the late date of the story of the encounter, there is another reason for looking upon it with suspicion as evidence of the date of Lao Tzu. When we examine this story we can see that it is, in fact, an illustrative story. It is, therefore, highly precarious to take the events contained in it as historical, particularly where the events concern only the variable factors.

In our story, the point is the discomfiture of Confucius in the hands of some hermit or other. The identity of the hermit, the location of the incident and the way the discomfiture is brought about are all variable factors. It is interesting to note that the accounts in the *Shih chi* are not in fact very close to the accounts about the encounter between Lao Tzu and Confucius in the *Chuang tʒu*, but resemble, in some features, rather more closely the account in the same work (chapter 26) of a meeting between Lao Lai Tzu – one of the persons with whom Lao Tzu is identified in his biography – and Confucius. This illustrates the point that the identity of the interlocutor is of little importance. Stories of this kind are to be found in more than one work, and one suspects that these originated with schools other than the Confucianist, in many cases probably Taoist. But some of these stories came to be accepted even by Confucianist circles at a fairly early date, as a few of them are to be found even in the *Analects of Confucius.** If we look upon these stories as forming a genre which must have been popular from fairly early times, then the fact that in a few of these the hermit happens to be Lao Tzu loses any historical significance it might have had they been unique. That a few illustrative stories of probably a late date are to be found in the *Chuang tʒu* is hardly sufficient evidence on which to rest the whole case for the historicity, let alone the early date, of Lao Tzu.

We cannot leave the present topic without taking at least a cursory glance at the passages in the *Li chi*. As we have seen, in these passages Confucius merely recounts what he heard from

---

* See the stories about the madman Chieh Yü of Ch'u, the tillers Ch'ang Chü and Chieh Ni, and the Old Man with the Basket (Book 18, sections 5 to 7).

Lao Tzu when he was with him. The Lao Tzu here is not a hermit who held Taoist views but an elderly gentleman well versed in the rites, as what Confucius learned from him concerned the finer points in their observance. The *Li chi* is a compilation of the first century B.C., and as we do not know from what sources these accounts were derived we can do no more than speculate about their date. My conjecture is that these were later in date than the stories in the Taoist tradition, and constituted a move on the part of the Confucians to counter the successful attempts by the Taoists to make Confucius a figure of ridicule. Instead of denying flatly that Confucius ever met Lao Tzu, or alternately, that Lao Tzu was a historical figure, they transformed him into an elderly gentleman well versed in the rites and so, in effect, turned him into a good Confucian. This was a very shrewd move, as it is far easier to change the nature of a widely accepted tradition than to discredit it altogether. That the move was successful can be seen from the fact that by the time Ssu-ma Ch'ien came to write the biographies of Lao Tzu and Confucius, he made use of Confucianist sources as well as the Taoist.

There is another tradition which is to be found in the biography of Lao Tzu in the *Shih chi*. This concerns his westward journey through the Pass and the writing of a work in two books at the request of the Keeper of the Pass (*kuan ling yin*). This story has no direct bearing on the date of Lao Tzu, but, nevertheless, it repays closer examination. Now at some time or other, after the story had gained wide acceptance, Kuan Yin*

---

* Kuan Yin, the Keeper of the Pass, is not to be confused with Kuan Yin, the bodhisattva in Chinese Buddhism. There is no connexion whatsoever between the two other than the accidental fact that their names, though totally different in Chinese, come out the same in romanized spelling.

(the Keeper of the Pass) came to be regarded as a philosopher in his own right, accredited with not only philosophical views but a philosophical work as well. It is interesting that Kuan Yin is mentioned in the *Lü shih ch'un ch'iu* (chüan 17, pt 7) as valuing 'limpidity'. He is also mentioned in the final chapter of the *Chuang tzu* which is a sort of general account of ancient Chinese thought and is considered by most scholars to be later in date than the main body of the work. In the *Chuang tzu*, Kuan Yin is mentioned in only one other chapter, chapter 19, but, again, there are some reasons for thinking that this chapter may be late as well. The *Hsün tzu*, for instance, mentions Lao Tzu's views once but not Kuan Yin, although, curiously enough, the notion of 'limpidity' figures prominently in a theory of the mind in chapter 21. This would seem to show that it was after the composition of the relevant parts of the *Hsün tzu* that Kuan Yin became an individual with a distinct identity.

Finally, there is one piece of evidence which is of some interest to us. In the *Yang chu* chapter of the *Lieh tzu*, there is recorded a conversation between Yang Chu and Ch'in Ku-li which ends with Ch'in Ku-li saying, 'If one were to ask Lao Tan and Kuan Yin about your opinion they would agree with you and if one were to ask the Great Yü and Mo Ti about mine, they would agree with me.' It is true, most scholars agree that the *Lieh tzu* is a late compilation, but much of the material in it is early and there is no reason to think that this story was an invention by the compiler. The point that concerns us is the apparent Mohist origin of the story. It seems hardly likely to be a pure coincidence that not only the tradition that Confucius received instruction from Lao Tzu had something to do with the Mohist school, but the name of Kuan Yin was also coupled with that of Lao Tzu in the words attributed to a well-known Mohist.

The tentative conclusion we have arrived at concerning Lao Tzu the man is this. There is no certain evidence that he was a historical figure. What is certain is that there are two stories about him, and concerning these there are two points worth noting. Firstly, both stories have something to do with the Mohist school; and secondly, both came to be widely known in the forty years or so before the compilation of the *Lü shih ch'un ch'iu* in 240 B.C. That in the *Lü shih ch'un ch'iu* the stories are taken for granted may be due to the fact that there probably was a Mohist among the editors. All this, and indeed my whole account of Lao Tzu, is speculative, but when there is so little that is certain there is not only room but need for speculation.

THE NATURE OF THE WORK

In the latter part of the Warring States period philosophical works no longer consisted of recorded sayings explicitly attributed to a particular thinker. The *Lao tzu* is no exception. Neither Lao Tzu nor the name of any other person appears in the work. That it is attributed to Lao Tzu is purely a matter of tradition.

Another feature of the works of this period is the increasing use of rhyming passages. In the case of the *Lao tzu* these amount to considerably more than half of the whole work. Such passages must have been meant to be learned by rote with the meaning explained at length in an oral commentary. Hence the cryptic nature of most of the sayings. As these rhyming passages were handed on orally, there probably was no one authoritative form nor one unique interpretation for them. They were common property to followers of various schools sharing a common tendency in thought.

There was, presumably, no one standard collection of such sayings either. This is confirmed by a cursory glance at the bibliographical chapter of the *Han shu*. Besides a work called *Lao lai tzu*, named after one of the figures with whom Lao Tzu was identified in the *Shih chi* biography, there are two works with titles that are interesting. These are the *Lao ch'eng tzu* and the *Cheng chang che*. Now *Lao ch'eng tzu* literally means 'the old man with mature wisdom' while *Cheng chang che* means 'the elder from the state of Cheng'. If we remember that *Lao tzu* literally means 'the old man' we cannot help being impressed

by the similarity of the titles of the three works. As far as I am
aware, we have no extant quotations from the *Lao ch'eng tzu*,
but fortunately for us there are preserved three quotations from
the *Cheng chang che* in the *Han fei tzu* (twice in chapter 34 and
once in chapter 37), and these bear a singular resemblance to
the *Lao tzu*. We can only conclude that in that period there
were a number of works which were Taoist in content, appearing
under various titles all of which meant 'old man' or 'elder', and
the important point for us is that the *Lao tzu* was only one of
these works. It so happened that Lao Tzu was also one of the
hermits that figured in the illustrative stories about Confucius.
The two facts reinforced each other so that the *Lao tzu* was
able to survive as the sole representative of this genre of literature, and, by the last quarter of the third century B.C., the work
was firmly associated with Lao Tzu, the man who was said to
have instructed Confucius in the rites.

Not only were there other collections similar to the *Lao tzu*,
but the *Lao tzu* itself probably did not exist in a definitive form
until a later period. In this respect, it is interesting to note that
in the *Huai nan tzu*, particularly in chapter 12, which uses
stories taken from various works as pegs for hanging quotations
from the *Lao tzu*, the text explicitly quoted as sayings of Lao
Tzu is practically identical with our present text. On the other
hand in the *Chieh Lao* (Explanations of Lao) and *Yü Lao* (Illus-
trations of Lao) chapters in the *Han fei tzu* where quotations are
never introduced by 'Lao Tzu said', though in a few cases by
'the Book said', the text is close to, but not identical with, the
present text, and quotations attributed to Lao Tzu in the final
chapter of the *Chuang tzu*, though in most cases recognizable as
such, differ considerably from the present text. It seems then

that the text was still in a fluid state in the second half of the third century B.C. or even later, but by the middle of the second century B.C., at the latest, the text already assumed a form very much like the present one. It is possible that this happened in the early years of the Western Han Dynasty. There is some reason to believe that in that period there were already specialist 'professors' (*po shih*) devoted to the study of individual ancient works, including the so-called philosophers (*chu tzu*), as distinct from the classics (*ching*). If that is the case, then the *Lao tzu* which was held in great esteem in court circles was almost certain to have its *po shih*. This would cause the text to become standardized and would also account for the fact that the text used by the editors of the *Huai nan tzu* was already, to all intents and purposes, identical with the present text.

It follows from what we have said about ancient Chinese works that they are best looked upon as anthologies. At best the material contained in such works consists of sayings of a particular thinker, often augmented by later material belonging to the same school. At worst the material is no more than a collection of passages with only a common tendency in thought. A careful reading of the *Lao tzu* cannot but leave us with the impression that it is not only an anthology but an anthology of the second kind. There are various features which give rise to such an impression.

Many chapters fall into sections having, at times, little or no connexion with one another. In the compilation of works of the latter part of the Warring States period one of the principles was the placing together of passages about the same topic which sometimes meant no more than passages having one or more catchwords in common. Whether this results in the putting together of passages which are relevant to one another depends on the purpose of the compiler which may be simply to facilitate memorization. This is true of the *Lao tzu*. If we do not bear this in mind and insist on treating chapters as organic wholes we run the risk of distorting the meaning. Two examples will make clear the kind of thing I have in mind. In chapter v we have

> Heaven and earth are ruthless, and treat the myriad creatures as straw dogs; the sage is ruthless, and treats the people as straw dogs. (14)

This is followed by

> Is not the space between heaven and earth like a bellows?
>   It is empty without being exhausted:
>   The more it works the more comes out. (15)

It is a different point that is made in each passage. In the first passage, the point is that heaven and earth are unfeeling, while in the second it is that they are inexhaustible though empty. There is no connexion between the two passages other than the fact that they are both about 'heaven and earth'.

Again, in chapter LXIV we find

> Whoever does anything to it will ruin it; whoever lays hold of it will lose it.
> Therefore the sage, because he does nothing, never ruins anything; and, because he does not lay hold of anything, loses nothing. (154, 154a)

This is followed by

> In their enterprises the people
> Always ruin them when on the verge of success.

> Be as careful at the end as at the beginning
> And there will be no ruined enterprises. (155)

Here we can see that the two passages have been placed together because they both deal with how things come to be ruined and how this can be avoided. But beyond this the point made in each passage is, once again, quite different. In the first passage, the sage avoids failure by not doing anything, while in the second the common people are exhorted to avoid failure when on the verge of success by being as careful at the end as at the beginning. In the one case, action is condemned as the cause of failure, because true success lies in not taking any action at all. In the other, it is assumed that success can be achieved through action, provided that one can be careful throughout the duration of the action. The two points of view are not simply unconnected; they are inconsistent.

Since passages which are placed together in the same chapter are very often unconnected or even inconsistent, many scholars in the past have felt dissatisfaction with the existing arrangement of the text, and some have even attempted to have the text rearranged. As these attempts seem to me to be based on mistaken assumptions, I have chosen to deal with the problem by a different method.*

In the *Lao tzu* the same passage is often to be found in different chapters. As the work is so short it is exceedingly unlikely that a single author should be so much given to repeating himself, but if we look upon the work as an anthology it is easier to see how this could have happened. Although in some cases one gets the impression that a passage which occurs

* See p. 51.

more than once fits better into one context than into another, in other cases it seems to fit equally well into the different contexts. This confirms the suggestion I made earlier regarding the probability that these passages existed as independent sayings with no fixed contexts. Again, in some cases it is clear that what is found in more than one chapter is really the same passage in a slightly different form. Incidentally, the recurrence of the same passage in different contexts often helps the reader to understand a text which, generally speaking, offers so little contextual aid.*

A few illustrative examples will make this clear. In chapter XVII we find

> When there is not enough faith, there is lack of good faith. (40)

This is found also in chapter XXIII (53). In neither case is this passage connected with its context. In fact it has more affinity with the passage in chapter XLIX which says

> Those who are of good faith I have faith in. Those who are lacking in good faith I also have faith in. In so doing I gain in good faith. (111)

We can see here that what is advocated is that we should extend our faith to even those who lack good faith. This is because by so doing we have some hopes of transforming them into men of good faith, whereas placing no faith in them will serve only to confirm them in their bad ways. Hence in a way the lack of good faith is the result of the lack of faith.

* On p. 145 a list is given of passages grouped for the purposes of comparison. Some groups consist of identical passages appearing in different contexts. Others consist of passages which, though not identical, may be profitably read together.

In contrast to the passage that does not seem to belong to any context, there is the passage which seems to belong to more than one. In chapter IV we have

> Blunt the sharpness;
> Untangle the knots;
> Soften the glare;
> Let your wheels move only along old ruts. (12)

In chapter LII we have

> Block the openings,
> Shut the doors,
> And all your life you will not run dry.
> Unblock the openings,
> Add to your troubles,
> And to the end of your days you will be beyond salvation.
> (118)

Yet in chapter LVI we find

> Block the openings;
> Shut the doors.
> Blunt the sharpness;
> Untangle the knots;
> Soften the glare;
> Let your wheels move only along old ruts. (129)

Faced with this, one's first reaction is to think that sections 12 and 118 are independent passages and that section 129 is a conflation of the two. This is probably the case, but one cannot be absolutely sure because sections 12 and 118 happen to share the same rhyme, and the two opening lines of section 12, moreover, happen to consist, like the lines in section 118, of three characters each.

We have seen that in chapter LXIV there is the passage

> Whoever does anything to it will ruin it; whoever lays hold of it will lose it. (154)

> Therefore the sage, because he does nothing, never ruins anything; and, because he does not lay hold of anything, loses nothing. (154a)

This passage does not have any connexion with either what follows or what goes before. Section 154 appears again in chapter XXIX:

> Whoever takes the empire and wishes to do anything to it I see will have no respite. The empire is a sacred vessel and nothing should be done to it. Whoever does anything to it will ruin it; whoever lays hold of it will lose it. (66)

Here a different context is given to the opening sentence. Whether this is, in any sense, the original context it is impossible to say, but it is at least more helpful to the understanding of the sentence than the obvious conclusion that 'the sage, because he does nothing, never ruins anything, and, because he does not lay hold of anything, loses nothing'.

Then there are cases where we find slightly different formulations of what is essentially the same passage. In chapter XXII we find

> He does not show himself, and so is conspicuous;
> He does not consider himself right, and so is illustrious;
> He does not brag, and so has merit;
> He does not boast, and so endures. (50b)

In chapter XXIV there is this,

> He who shows himself is not conspicuous;
> He who considers himself right is not illustrious;
> He who brags will have no merit;
> He who boasts will not endure. (55)

It is obvious that these two passages are simply the positive and negative ways of saying the same thing.

Take another case. In chapter LXX we find

> My words are very easy to understand and very easy to put into practice, yet no one in the world can understand them or put them into practice. (170)

In chapter LXXVIII we have

> That the weak overcomes the strong,
> And the submissive overcomes the hard,
> Everyone in the world knows yet no one can put this knowledge into practice. (187)

Here we have not only a different formulation of the same saying, but also an apparent difference in substance. In section 170 it is said that '*no one* in the world can understand', while in section 187 it is said that '*everyone* in the world knows'. The difference, however, is more apparent than real. What the sage says is really very easy to understand, and in a sense everyone understands it, but it is because the truth is so simple and easy to understand that the clever people tend to find it ridiculous. But the difference between those who understand and those who do not is unimportant, because they are alike in their inability to act on the moral contained in the words. This seems to show that the same saying, in the process of oral transmission, assumed slightly different forms in different contexts while retaining essentially the same moral.

The work then is an anthology, compiled by more than one hand, and there are at least three ways in which the existing material has been dealt with. Firstly, two or more pre-existing passages are joined together. This is too common to need examples. Secondly, a pre-existing passage is followed by a passage of exposition. A good example is section 30 and 30a in chapter XIII. Thirdly, a pre-existing passage is preceded by a passage of exposition. Section 191 in chapter LXXIX is an example. In cases of the last two types, it frequently happens that the pre-existing passage is in rhyme, while the exposition that is added is in prose, but it also sometimes happens that the exposition added is so contrived as to rhyme with the original passage. Section 7a is a particularly interesting example, because, by rhyming *chü* with *ch'ü*, the editor was in fact revealing that he pronounced *chü* in a way different from the way it was pronounced when section 7 was composed.

In all these cases, the clue to the editing lies often in the use of connectives like *ku* (therefore, thus) and *shih yi* (hence). Naturally, these words are often used in their proper function as links in a consecutive argument, but more often they are to be found precisely where the logical link is weakest. A careful reading of the texts of the latter part of the Warring States period with an eye to the continuity of argument will confirm the impression that these words were used to connect passages which have in fact little or no connexion. There is one clear example of these words being deliberately put to such a use in the *Huai nan tzu*. Chapter 12 of this work consists of a collection of stories each culminating in a quotation from the *Lao tzu*. The quotations in most cases are from a single chapter of the existing text, but in three cases the quotations are from two different chapters. Instead of having the quotation from each chapter preceded by the formula 'Lao Tzu said', a single formula serves to introduce both quotations which are separated by the word *ku*. It seems that the editors of the *Huai nan tzu* were still aware of the editorial function of such words and used them as an indication to the reader that the two parts of the same quotation were in fact from different chapters of the *Lao tzu*.

One type of editorial comment stands out very clearly. There are certain set formulae that are used more than once. For instance, chapters XII, XXXVIII, and LXXII all end with the line

> Therefore he discards the one and takes the other.

Again, chapters XXI and LIV and the opening section in chapter LVII all end with the line

> How do I know that . . . is (or are) like that? By means of this.

On the question of the date of the work it is not possible to arrive at an exact answer. As we have seen, there is reason to believe that there were similar collections in the Warring States attributed to other wise old men, and that there were probably different versions of the *Lao tzu* at one time, though by the beginning of the Han Dynasty the text was already very much the same as the text we have at present. It also seems to be clear that the text must have existed for some time before then, for we find a highly esoteric interpretation in the *Chieh Lao* chapter in the *Han fei tzu* which was probably somewhat earlier than the *Huai nan tzu*, as the text quoted in it from the *Lao tzu* diverges to a greater extent from our present text. As to how long a period is needed for a tradition of esoteric interpretation to grow up, this is a question to which there is no ready answer.

Taking all factors into account, I am inclined to the hypothesis that some form of the *Lao tzu* existed by the beginning of the third century B.C. at the latest. This is supported to a certain extent by the fact that in the *Lao tzu* are to be found many ideas which were associated with a number of thinkers of the second half of the fourth and the first quarter of the third century B.C. The general impression one gains in reading the *Lao tzu* is that it was the product of this same golden period which produced so many great thinkers many of whom congregated at Chi Hsia in the state of Ch'i during the second half of the fourth century B.C. This does not, of course, mean that the *Lao tzu* does not contain some material which is much earlier than this period. It has, for instance, been often pointed out that the line

> Do good to him who has done you an injury,

in chapter LXIII was already treated as a common saying in the *Analects of Confucius* (14. 36). Again, a passage very similar to section 79 in chapter XXXVI is attributed in both the *Han fei tzu* and the *Chan kuo ts'e* to a work called the *Book of Chou* and quoted as from a poem in the *Lü shih ch'un ch'iu*. In a work of this nature it is not surprising that it should contain material that ranges over a wide period of time.

CHRONOLOGICAL TABLE

EASTERN CHOU DYNASTY, 770–256 B.C.

  A The Spring and Autumn Period, 722–481 B.C.

     *Confucius, 551–479 B.C.

  B The Warring States Period, 480–222 B.C.

     *Mo Tzu, *fl.* fifth century B.C.

     Yang Chu, *fl.* fourth century B.C.

     *Mencius, *fl.* fourth century B.C.

     Sung K'eng (and Yin Wen), second quarter to end of fourth century B.C.

     Shen Tao (and T'ien P'ien), middle of fourth to first quarter of third century B.C.

     *Chuang Tzu, middle of fourth to beginning of third century B.C.

     *Hsün Tzu, latter half of fourth to middle of third century B.C.

     The *Lü shih ch'un ch'iu*, postface dated 240 B.C.

     *Han Fei Tzu, d. 233 B.C.

CH'IN DYNASTY, 221–207 B.C.

WESTERN HAN DYNASTY, 206 B.C.–A.D. 8

     The *Huai nan tzu*, compiled *c.* 140 B.C.

     Ssu-ma Ch'ien, the *Shih chi*, completed *c.* 90 B.C.

     The *Li chi*, compiled by Tai Sheng (*fl.* first century B.C.)

     Liu Hsiang, the *Hsin hsü* and the *Shuo yüan*, presented to the throne *c.* 16 B.C.

WANG MANG, A.D. 9–23

EASTERN HAN DYNASTY, A.D. 25–220

     Pan Ku (A.D. 32–92), the *Han shu*

---

* Thinkers with extant works attributed to them or their disciples, and, with the exception of Confucius, named after them.

GLOSSARY

BOOK OF CHANGES. Although this is numbered among the Thirteen Confucian Classics, it was, in its basic text, originally no more than a manual for divination by the method of the hexagrams. A hexagram, which is made up of two trigrams, is a figure consisting of six lines, one placed above another. As there are two kinds of lines, the broken and the continuous, the total number of possible hexagrams is sixty-four. There is a text on each hexagram which explains the prognosticatory significance both of the hexagram as a whole and the individual lines. But from very early times, attempts were made to read a philosophical significance into this system. This is the purpose of some of the commentaries, commonly known as 'the ten wings'. The broken line is taken to represent the *yin* and the continuous the *yang*, and the *yin* and the *yang* are looked upon as the basic forces in the universe which wax and wane alternately and relative to each other, thus giving rise to a cyclic process of change. An obvious instance of this process is the four seasons. In summer the *yang* force is at its highest and the *yin* at its lowest while in autumn the *yang* is on the decline and the *yin* on the rise. In winter the state of affairs is the reverse of that in summer, and that in spring the reverse of that in autumn.

BOOK OF HISTORY. Also one of the Thirteen Confucian Classics. This is the earliest extant collection of historical documents. The present text consists of 58 chapters. Of these 33 chapters which are equivalent to 28 of the so-called 'modern script' text are considered genuine while the rest are very late forgeries compiled out of ancient material. The period of history covered ranges from Yao who was one of the legendary kings to the Chou Dynasty.

BOOK OF ODES. Another of the Thirteen Confucian Classics. It is the earliest collection of poems, some three hundred in all, that were composed in the five centuries or so before the time of Confucius. The work is divided into three parts, the *feng*, the *ya*, and the *sung*. The *feng* consists of folk songs of the various states; the *ya* consists of songs sung at court during banquets and entertainment of guests; and the *sung* consists of songs in praise of imperial ancestors sung on sacrificial occasions.

CHANKUO TS'E (*The Stratagems of the Warring States*). In the Warring States period there was a large class of political adventurers who travelled from one state to another offering advice to the rulers. This work is a collection of such strategems arranged under the various states, which has come down to us in a version edited by Liu Hsiang. It is not certain when the work was first compiled, but there is a view that this was done at the beginning of the Han Dynasty.

CHI HSIA. In the Warring States period wandering scholars and political advisers attained a much higher status than in the preceding period, and it became fashionable for feudal lords to gather them at their courts. One of the most famous of such gatherings was at Chi Hsia in the state of Ch'i. The Chi gate was the western gate of the capital of Ch'i, and Chi Hsia simply means 'under the Chi gate'. The scholars gathered there for discussions and it is said that an academy was built there for that purpose. Chi Hsia was at the height of its fame under King Wei (356–320 B.C.) and King Hsüan (319–301 B.C.), though it probably began before then and certainly was revived at the time of King Hsiang (283–265 B.C.) when Hsün Tzu was the most senior among the scholars. Many of the brilliant thinkers of the period were at one time or another at Chi Hsia. It is interesting to note that, though he was in Ch'i during the time of King Hsüan, Mencius never was numbered amongst the scholars of Chi Hsia.

CHOU. The name of the Dynasty which lasted from 1027 to 256 B.C., with its capital transferred to Loyang in 770. By the Spring and Autumn period, however, the Chou emperor was no more than the titular head of the empire and his territory was no bigger than that of a minor state. It was to Loyang that Confucius was supposed to have gone to seek the instruction of Lao Tzu.

CONFUCIUS (551–479 B.C.). Confucius was brought up in humble circumstances but was, from an early age, known for his learning. Though he had ambitions of attaining a position of political influence, he never succeeded in realizing this ambition and his life was spent in teaching. The importance of Confucius lies in his being the first great teacher as well as philosopher. In denying no one acceptance as a disciple provided that he was genuinely eager to learn, he probably did more than anyone in preventing education from becoming the exclusive privilege of the aristocracy. He was the first philosopher to whom a collection of sayings is attributed which is, on the whole, reliable. This is the *Lun yü* or the *Analects of Confucius* as it is commonly known in English.

CHUANG TZU. We know very little about Chuang Tzu. According to the *Shih chi*, his given name was Chou and he was a contemporary of King Hui (369–319 B.C.) of Wei and King Hsüan of Ch'i. It is also said that his thought was derived from that of Lao Tzu. The *Chuang tʒu* is certainly a very mixed collection. Some of the earliest chapters probably represent the thought of Chuang Tzu while the later chapters probably belong to the Ch'in or even the early Han period. Although Chuang Tzu is always mentioned with Lao Tzu as the other great Taoist thinker, the thought in the more representative parts of the *Chuang tʒu* differs considerably from that of the *Lao tʒu*. Two points in the thought of the *Chuang tʒu* are particularly interesting. Firstly, judgements about right and wrong are said to be always made from a point of view, so that not only are different judgements made concerning the same things from different points of view but also it is impossible to decide on the relative merits of these different standpoints. As a solution, the *Chuang tʒu* suggests a higher point of view which is impartial in its attitude towards all the possible points of view. These are treated as equally valid or, if you like, equally invalid. It follows that life is desirable and death undesirable only from the point of view of the living. How then does one know that the reverse is not the case from the point of view of the dead? The result is the position that there is no reason to prefer one view to another. Secondly, the *Chuang tʒu* shows great interest in the problem of whether there is something which is in effective control over mental activities such as sense-perception. This 'mind' or 'soul' which is the elusive sovereign of the body seems to be thought of as a counterpart to the '*tao*' which is the equally elusive sovereign of the universe.

HAN FEI TZU. Han Fei Tzu was a member of the royal house of the state of Han. He was said to have studied under Hsün Tzu at the same time as Li Ssu who subsequently became the prime minister of Ch'in. When Han was on the verge of collapse in face of the attack by Ch'in, Han Fei was sent as envoy to Ch'in. Though the king of Ch'in was pleased with him, he was said to have died as a result of the machinations of Li Ssu, who was jealous of his superior talent. In his thought Han Fei combined the teachings of a number of schools to form the system known as Legalist thought. It combined 'the methods of dealing with the subjects' advocated by Shen Pu-hai, 'the rule of law' advocated by Lord Shang and 'the exploitation of the vantage position of the ruler' advocated by Shen Tao. Some Taoist ideas are also given a Legalist interpretation.

HAN SHU. Pan Piao began the *Han shu* but died before he could complete it. His son Pan Ku carried on and all but finished the work. It covered the history of the Western Han Dynasty to Wang Mang. The bibliographical chapter of the *Han shu* is of the greatest interest and importance to students of ancient Chinese literature. Most of the ancient works came down to posterity through the recension of Liu Hsiang who was entrusted with the task of editing the books in the Imperial library. His son Liu Hsin (d. A.D. 23) made a catalogue of these books under the title of the *Ch'i lüeh* (*The Seven Summaries*). This is no longer extant, but fortunately we have the *Han shu* bibliographical chapter which was based on the *Ch'i lüeh*, and it is to this chapter that we owe most of our information about the books in the ancient period.

HSÜN TZU. After Mencius, the most important name in the Confucian school. From the *Hsün tʐu* we can see that the most important points in his teaching are these. Human nature is evil. This means that if men were to follow the dictates of their nature, the result can only be conflict and disorder. As a solution to this problem the sage-kings invented morality. Since morality has no basis in his nature, the only way of making man moral is by sheer habituation. Hsün Tzu draws a clear distinction between what pertains to heaven and what pertains to man. Under the influence of the Taoists, heaven in the *Hsün tʐu* became no more than Nature in its regularity, which is no longer looked upon as having a moral purpose. The greatest contribution of Hsün Tzu lies in his realization that if heaven is nothing but the regular workings of Nature man should no longer model his way of life on Nature but should work out his own salvation. Hence the importance of the clear understanding of the difference between 'heaven' and 'man'.

HUAI NAN TZU. Liu An, a grandson of the first emperor of the Han Dynasty, was made Prince of Huai Nan in 164 B.C., ten years after his father, who held the same title, starved himself to death on being banished by Emperor Wen for his part in an unsuccessful rebellion. Liu An, following in the footsteps of his father, cast covetous eyes on the Imperial throne and when his plot came to light committed suicide (in 122 B.C.) rather than face the death sentence. The *Huai nan tʐu* was compiled by scholars he gathered around him at his court. Its value and that of the *Lü shih ch'un ch'iu* before it cannot be put too high. When most ancient Chinese works are of uncertain date, these two stand out as landmarks of certainty. Moreover, the views of earlier thinkers whose works are no longer extant are often incorporated in these two works. In this respect, the *Huai nan tzu* is even more important than its predecessor, which it surpasses in philosophical interest. This rich mine of information has, however, scarcely been tapped.

KUAN TZU. A work attributed to Kuan Chung, the most illustrious statesman in the Spring and Autumn period through whose efforts Duke Huan of Ch'i (685–643 B.C.) became the acknowledged leader of the feudal lords, but in fact a collection of heterogeneous materials which vary widely in nature as well as in date.

LIEH TZU. Lieh Tzu is a rather nebulous figure, and the present work named after him is a late compilation, though the compiler made use of a great deal of material which was genuinely early. The argument from the existence of Lieh Tzu who is himself problematical to that of Lao Tzu is of no value at all.

LÜ SHIH CH'UN CH'IU. A work compiled by the scholars in the service of Lü Pu-wei, the prime minister of Ch'in from 249 to 237 B.C., with a postface dated 240 B.C. It was meant to be a compendium of all knowledge that mattered and is therefore a useful source for the views of schools of thought whose representative works are no longer extant.

MENCIUS. The most illustrious thinker in the Confucian school. Like Confucius, he spent many years travelling in different states trying to persuade rulers to follow his philosophy but met with little success. He is best known for his theory that human nature is good. This means that man is born with the ability to distinguish between right and wrong, naturally approves of the former and disapproves of the latter and feels ashamed when he fails to do what is his duty. This aimed, on the one hand, at countering the theory current in his day that human nature consists merely of appetites and, on the other, at re-interpreting the traditional view subscribed to by the Confucians that morality was decreed by heaven. Mencius successfully broke down the rigid distinction and opposition between human nature and heavenly decree. Morality is as much part of human nature as appetites, and appetites are as much part of heavenly decree as morality. Another of the views of Mencius is worth noting. The function of the ruler is the furtherance of the good of the people. If a ruler tyrannizes over the people he is no longer a ruler but just 'a fellow' and the people have the right to revolution.

Mo Tzu. We know very little about Mo Tzu. From the *Shih chi* we learn only that his given name was Ti and his surname was Mo, that he was an officer of the state of Sung and was, according to one view, contemporary with, but according to another later than, Confucius. The most basic tenet of his teachings is 'love without discrimination' which is the 'will of heaven'. He was an extreme utilitarian. Everything that is of no obvious utility to the people is to be given up. This includes war, elaborate burial, prolonged mourning, and the performance of music. He was a considerable mechanic and was able to devise tools of defensive warfare. One extremely interesting part of the *Mo tzu* is the six chapters devoted to the discussion of topics of a scientific and logical nature. These probably belonged to a later period but there is no doubt that they were the work of the Mohist school. Unfortunately, the text, through centuries of neglect, is exceedingly corrupt.

THE PASS. In the story of the westward journey of Lao Tzu the Pass he was supposed to have gone through has been variously identified as the Han Ku Pass and the San Pass, but it is most probably the former which is to the south of Ling Pao Hsien in the modern province of Honan.

SHIH CHI. Ssu-ma Ch'ien succeeded his father as official Historian in 108 B.C. at the age of thirty-eight, and devoted himself to the preparation of material for the writing of a general history of China, as this was the unrealized ambition of his father. This resulted in the *Shih chi* which he finished about 90 B.C. after he had suffered the most humiliating punishment at the hands of Emperor Wu in 98 B.C. This work has exercised tremendous influence on subsequent historiography. It set the pattern for all the later so-called 'official histories'. The *Shih chi* consists mainly of biographies, though it contains a number of tables and there are chapters on various general topics like 'rites', 'the calendar', 'astronomy', 'irrigation', and 'public finance'. He drew on a large number of works, archives of his own office and oral tradition which he diligently collected in his travels. In cases where he was able to judge he chose what he believed to be reliable. But he did not reject what was no more than doubtful where he had no grounds for choice. This would account for the inclusion of so much legend in the biography of Lao Tzu.

SUNG K'ENG. The only thing we know for certain about Sung K'eng's views is to be found in the *Hsün tzu*. He is there represented as saying that man does not by nature desire a great deal. As strife is the result of covetousness, if only men could be brought to realize that they do not in fact desire a great deal, there would be no strife. He also believes that there is no disgrace in being insulted. People fight because they feel disgraced, and if they could realize that there is no disgrace in being insulted, they would not be inclined to fight. These views seem rather paradoxical, but these might not have been presented in their best light by the *Hsün tzu* which is critical of them. At any rate, they do show that there is some affinity between the views of Sung Keng and the austere and pacifist views held by the Mohists.

TAOISM. The English term 'Taoism' is ambiguous. It is used to translate both the Chinese term '*tao chia* (the school of the *tao*)' and '*tao chiao* (the Taoist religion)'. In the present work, Taoism is used only in the former sense, though the more popular schools of Taoist thought in the early Han probably had considerable affinity with the views of the later devotees of the Taoist religion which came into being towards the end of the Eastern Han.

TE. Apart from the special Taoist use of the word (see p. 42), the word has a number of conventional meanings. Firstly, it means 'moral virtue'; secondly, it means 'bounty'; thirdly, it means 'to be grateful' or 'to be conscious that others ought to be grateful to oneself'.

T'IEN. This term means both 'heaven' and the 'skies'. Because of this, there is a tendency in Chinese thought not to distinguish the two.

WANG PI (A.D. 226–49). A brilliant thinker who, in spite of the fact that he died at the early age of twenty-three, has exercised tremendous influence on subsequent thought. He has left a commentary on the *Book of Changes* and one on the *Lao tzu*. In the former he gave a philosophical, rather than numerological, interpretation, and this commentary of his was accepted into the corpus of 'official commentaries' on the Confucian classics in T'ang times. His commentary on the *Lao tzu* is equally important because it is the earliest extant philosophical commentary of the work. He is also responsible for the tendency to find an affinity between the two works.

YIN, YANG. It is probable that the two terms originally meant 'sunless' and 'sunny'. For instance, the southern side of a mountain is *yang* and the northern side *yin*, while the southern side of a river is *yin* and the northern side *yang*. Then they came to mean 'female' and 'male'. Finally, they became general terms for the fundamental and opposite forces or principles of nature. In the commentaries of the *Book of Changes*, *yang* was used to describe the continuous, and *yin* the broken, line in a hexagram. The fact that *yin* and *yang* became important philosophical terms is not unconnected with the fact that at the same time the *Book of Changes* was transformed from a manual for divination to a work of profound philosophical significance.

NOTES

I

1. Read 暾.

II

1. Read 形.
2. Take 辭 as a loan for 司. See Kao Heng, *Lao tzu cheng ku*, pp. 7–8.

IV

1. Emend 盈 to 窮.
2. For this interpretation of the line, cf. the line '比迹 同塵' in the poem *Tseng Feng Wen-p'i ch'ien Ch'ih-ch'iu ling* by Lu Chi (see the *Wen hsüan*, chüan 24). It is obvious that Lu Chi treats the two phrases as synonymous.

V

1. Read 中 as 沖. I owe this suggestion to Professor Hsü Fu-kuan.

VIII

1. It is probable that this line is an interpolation. Of the seven lines in this section, this is the only one that fails to rhyme. If this line is removed, the remaining lines fall neatly into two sets of three rhyming lines.

IX

1. For a detailed discussion of the vessel, see my article 'On the term "*ch'ih ying*" and the story concerning the so-called "tilting vessel"', *Symposium on Chinese Studies commemorating the Golden Jubilee of the University of Hong Kong 1911–1961*, Vol. III, 1968, Hong Kong.

X

1. Read 載 as 戴.
2. Read 無為.
3. Read 為雌.
4. Read 無知.

XV

1. Read 道.
2. Read 客.
3. Read 以止.
4. Read 蔽 as 敝.

XVI

1. The passage beginning with 'to kingliness' seems to be an interpolation as it has no rhymes.

XVII

1. Read 悠 as 猶. For this meaning of *yu*, see the line 'Hesitant, as if in fear of his neighbours' (section 35).

XVIII

1. Take 慈 as synonymous with 孝. Kao is most probably right in thinking that the text should read 孝孫, as this line should rhyme with the last line in the chapter (op cit., pp. 42–3).

XIX

1. See the first sentence of the previous note.
2. Read 為 as 偽.

XX

1. Read 遺 as 匱.

XXI

1. Transpose 古 and 今 for the sake of the rhyme.
2. Read 然.

XXIII

    1. Omit 者.

XXIV

    1. Read 形.

XXVI

    1. Read 君子.
    2. Read 雖 as 唯.
    3. Read 榮 as 營.

XXX

    1. Read 者.
    2. Emend 則 to 賊.

XXXI

    1. Emend 佳 to 唯.

XXXVIII

    1. Read 不爲 in both cases.

XXXIX

    1. Insert 一 也.
    2. Read 爲 貞.
    3. Omit 數, and read 輿 as 譽.

XLI

    1. Emend 眞 to 德.
    2. Read 善 成.

XLIII

    1. It is probable that the text should read 事 instead
    of 益, in which case the translation should read 'the
    deed that consists in no action'. Cf. section 6.

XLVI

1. Insert 罪 莫 大 於 多 欲, following the reading in the *Han shih wai chuan*.

2. Omit 之 足.

XLVII

1. Although it makes no difference to the sense, the reading should probably be 毖 because of the rhyme.

2. There seems to be a line missing with which this line rhymes.

XLIX

1. Insert 百 姓 皆 注 其 耳 目.

L

1. Read 人 之 生 生 而 動 之 死 地.

LI

1. Omit 德.

LII

1. Read 可 以.

2. Read 習 as 襲. Cf. '襲 明 (following one's discernment)' in section 61a.

LV

1. Read 毒 蟲.

2. Judging from the internal rhyme, '之 合 (the union of)' must have been a gloss which crept into the text.

3. Read 朘, or, alternately, take 全 as a corruption of 㑹, as suggested by Yü Yüeh.

LIX

1. This, in line with the next line, should read '有 國 之 母 (the possession of the mother of the state)' as well.

LXI

1. Read 交 instead of 牝.

2. Transfer 欲 to after 各. Although this does not make any substantial difference to the sense, it restores the rhyme with the next line. This is borne out by the wording of the Ho Shang commentary.

LXII

1. Read 美 行.

LXIV

1. There seems to be a line missing with which this line rhymes.

LXV

1. Omit 知.

LXVIII

1. Omit 古.

LXIX

1. In view of the rhyme, this line should probably come immediately after 'This is known as' as suggested by Kao (op. cit., p. 139).

LXXV

1. Omit 上 and read 生 生 for 求 生.

LXXVI

1. Omit 萬物.

2. These two lines are quoted in the *Huang ti* chapter of the *Lieh tzu* and the *Yüan tao* chapter of the *Huai nan tzu* as

A weapon when strong is destroyed;
A tree when strong is felled.

But in view of the rhyme between 兵 and 上 there is no reason to suppose that the *Lao tzu* text should be emended according to the other two works.

LXXVIII

1. Read 以其.

LAO TZU
TAO TE CHING

TRANSLATED BY D. C. LAU

The *Lao Tzu*, as it is usually called, is the principal classic in the thought of Taoism. Traditionally ascribed to one Lao Tzu, 'an older contemporary of Confucius, the work is more probably an anthology of wise sayings compiled in about the fourth century B.C. As a treatise both on personal conduct and on government it is moral rather than mystical in tone, and advances a philosophy of meekness as the surest path to survival. In the clear English of D. C. Lau's new translation this famous Chinese book can be enjoyed especially for its pure poetry.

The cover illustration shows a detail from a Chinese silk painting in the British Museum

Penguin  Classics